Sandstone Depositional Models
For Exploration For Fossil Fuels

George deVries Klein
Professor of Sedimentology

University of Illinois
at Urbana-Champaign

Continuing Education Publication Company, Inc
P O Box 2590 Station A   Champaign, IL 61820

Printed in the United States of America

Second Printing: February, 1977

Library of Congress Catalog Card Number: 76-359291

ISBN: 0-89469-083-3

ACKNOWLEDGMENTS

This short course syllabus is an outgrowth of several short courses I have presented dealing with sandstone models and exploration. The stimulus for preparing the syllabus came from Dr. Ram S. Saxena, Chairman of the Continuing Education Committee of the New Orleans Geological Society, who invited me to present this course in 1974 and requested that I prepare a syllabus for it. I would like to take this opportunity to thank Dr. Saxena for his encouragement and assistance during that visit to New Orleans. This present syllabus is a revised version of the earlier syllabus and includes a new chapter.

I also wish to thank the American Association of Petroleum Geologists for inviting me to serve as a continuing education lecturer in their program on Continuing Education. Through their assistance in many ways, and through their encouragement, this revision of the syllabus was completed. I particularly want to thank Mrs. Judy Golasinski, Lecturer Coordinator, for her unending patience and willingness to assist me during my various travels as an AAPG Continuing Education Lecturer. I also thank Dr. Howard R. Gould, Chairman of the AAPG Continuing Education Committee, for inviting me to participate in their program activities.

Permission to reprint illustrations was granted by the University of Chicago Press, the International Association of Sedimentologists, the Geological Society of America, the Netherlands Geological and Mining Society, the Geological Society of Italy, the American Association of Petroleum Geologists, the Society for Economic Paleontologists and Mineralogists, the American Journal of Science, the Society of Exploration Geophysicists, Dowden, Hutchinson and Ross, Inc., and John Wiley and Sons, Inc. I am extremely grateful to these organizations for their assistance. I also wish to thank the many authors who also granted me permission to reprint their illustrations; appropriate acknowledgement to them is given in the figure captions.

Finally, I wish to thank the many past participants in this short course whose stimulating and probing questions helped focus many of the concepts and text presented in this syllabus.

George deVries Klein
Urbana, Illinois.
October, 1975

Cover Photo: The illustration on the cover is taken from D.G. Moore's paper entitled "Relection profiling studies of the California continental borderland: structure and Quaternary Turbidite basins" which was published as Geol. Soc. America Spec. Paper 107 (his figure 22, p. 72). It is reprinted by permission of D.G. Moore and the Geological Society of America.

TABLE OF CONTENTS

INTRODUCTION

The purpose of this syllabus is to provide participants in my AAPG Continuing Education Short Course with an outline of the material I cover in my lectures. In addition, some of the illustrative material is reproduced for guidance. A brief bibliography of reference material that I consider to be critical to my remarks is added to each chapter, although no claim for topical completeness is made.

In addition, this syllabus is intended as a brief summary of the depositional processes, Holocene sediments, ancient counterparts and examples of stratigraphic traps in five depositional environments. This summary is intended to complement lecture and reading courses dealing with depositional systems, sedimentary environments and sedimentary modelling as a predictive tool for exploration. The student is cautioned, however, that this syllabus is merely an introduction and summary overview of the subject. More complete treatments are covered in standard textbooks.

The emphasis of this syllabus is the understanding of five types of sandstone depositional models which are proven to contain reservoirs of petroleum and natural gas, and also to contain uranium deposits. These five types are:

(1)   Fluvial Sand Body Model
(2)   Beach and Barrier Island Sand Body Model
(3)   Tidal Flat and Tidal Sand Body Model
(4)   Deltaic Sand Body Model
(5)   Turbidite Sand Body Model.

In this syllabus, both the geological and geophysical criteria that will permit recognition of such sand bodies as potential stratigraphic traps for exploitation and production are developed. The outline to be followed is relatively simple. Each section begins with a discussion of Holocene sediment deposition processes where such sand bodies evolve. Next, the sedimentary criteria and geometry of each of these sand bodies will be reviewed from Holocene sediment data. Third, examples of ancient counterpart sandstone bodies will be presented. Each section closes with a very brief review of examples of oil field and uranium deposit case histories. Electric log and seismic characteristics of some of these sand bodies are reviewed in the applied section of each chapter.

The models reviewed here are of world-wide occurrence and importance for hydrocarbon and uranium exploration, and although the majority of examples discussed are from North America, readers of this syllabus should be able to find many additional examples in their own areas. Such examples should permit them to consider new and different concepts for the exploration and production of undiscovered oil and gas fields.

1

FLUVIAL SAND BODIES

INTRODUCTION

The sediments of fluvial systems have interested geologists for many years. A large literature has grown around fluvial processes (summarized in Leopold et al, 1964), fluvial sediments (See Allen, 1965 for a review) and facies models. Fluvial sands contain petroleum (Nanz, 1954; Harms, 1966; MacKenzie, 1972) and also form host rocks for the well-known sandstone-type uranium deposits documented from the Rocky Mountain region.

Of the various types of sediments to be reviewed in this syllabus, the fluvial sediments show the greatest range of textural variability. In particular, the sediment sorting is highly variable; most being poor. Nevertheless, in certain cases, particularly with fluvial systems on coastal plains, sorting improves and such fluvial sandstones contain excellent petroleum reservoir characteristics.

ALLUVIAL FANS

Alluvial fans occur in both arid and humid regions where a sharp reduction in depositional slope occurs. The best development of alluvial fans occurs, therefore, along fault scarps and fault-line scarps. The alluvial fan form owes its origin to sudden reduction in open channel flow velocity on encountering a sudden reduction in slope angle. Both morphology and sediment distribution is controlled by these slope changes (Figure 1 and 2). Shifting drainage patterns permit fans to form a sheet-like bajada marginal to a mountain front (Denny, 1967; figure 3).

Alluvial Fan Processes

Several depositional processes occur on alluvial fans. The discussion follows those by Hooke (1967, 1968), Denny (1967), Bull (1972) and Spearing (1975). The major processes active on a fan include debris flow, sieve deposition, braided channel systems and wind reworking.

Debris Flow: Debris flow is common to alluvial fans, particularly in arid zones, and also on submarine fans. This process is discussed in the last chapter dealing with turbidites and the reader is referred to it for a detailed discussion.

Sieve Deposition: Hooke (1967) has demonstrated that on arid alluvial fans, many of the sediment surfaces are highly porous. Consequently, it is not unusual that some of the water which transport sediments filters through the porous zone and leaves behind a lobe of sediment which is stranded by such infiltration (Figure 4). This sediment lobe is very poorly sorted, and contains sediment sizes ranging from boulder to clay. The lobes occur as linear sediment bodies (Figure 1 and 2), confined mostly to the apical fan zone, and are oriented approximately parallel to depositional strike.

Braided Channels: Braided channel systems tend to be superimposed on alluvial fan surfaces in response to moderate to higher slope angles characterisitc of alluvial fans. Because of the rapid change in flow velocity of the channels debauching onto the fan, sediment dumping is rapid and water tends to flow around such depositional sites and become arranged into a system of braided streams. These streams bifurcate and build local islands between channels. The braided channels are characterized by shallow depths relative to channel width, and new braids are generated as further sediment deposition of bars occurs in response to sudden changes in flow velocity.

Wind Reworking: On arid alluvial fans, resedimentation of fine- and medium-grained sand by wind systems is common.

Alluvial Fan Sediments and Facies

Morphologically and sedimentologically, alluvial fans are subdivided into a proximal, medial and distal facies (Figure 1 and 5.).

Proximal Facies: The proximal facies is characterized by the highest depositional slope angles and occur adjacent to a fault scarp or fault-line scarp in the fan's apical zone. The sediment there consists of extremely poorly-sorted gravels which lack a fabric. Stratification features are non-existent. The grain-supported gravel is bound by clay, silt and sand.

Medial Facies: The medial facies consists of interbedded sand and gravel. The sand/gravel ratio increases when compared with that of the proximal facies. Gravel clasts are also imbricated. Sand is parallel-laminated and may also contain antidune cross-stratification (Hand et al, 1969). Sediment sorting is improved with respect to the proximal facies, but it is still poor. Local thin channel zones with cross-stratified fill occurs in response to braided stream action. This facies occurs within the middle portion of an alluvial fan and is characterized by a medium to lower angle of despositional slope.

Distal Facies: This facies occurs at the toe of an alluvial fan, an area characterized by the lowest angle of depositional slope. Here, the sediment consists dominantly of sand or gravelly sand. The sediment shows fair sorting. Structures present include parallel laminae, cross-stratification and imbricated gravel clasts. Channel fills of braided channels are common in this faces.

Alluvial Fan Vertical Sequence.

The vertical sequence of alluvial fans tends to be a coarsening-upward sequence (Wessel, 1969). Within each of the fan zones, specific sequences can be documented (Figure 5). Fan progradation displaces the proximal facies over the medial facies and the medial facies over the distal facies, accounting for such a sequence. Depositional events also favor the development of local coarsening-upward sequences (Figure 6) which show a succession of structures consisting of ripples, parallel laminae, antidune cross-strata and massive conglomerates (Figure 6) reflecting a local increase in flow intensity and possibly also of sediment concentration by the depositional system of fluvial flow and debris flow.

Ancient Examples of Alluvial Fans

Ancient alluvial fan facies have been documented in several fossil examples. Excellent examples include the Devonian of Norway (Nilsen, 1969; see Figure 7), the Carboniferous of the Maritime Provinces of Canada (Belt, 1968), the Triassic of Wales (Bluck, 1965), the Triassic of Nova Scotia (Klein, 1962), the Triassic of Massachusetts (Wessel, 1969; Hand et al, 1969), and the Neogene Violin Breccia of California (Crowell, 1974). In the Triassic of Massachusetts, the Mt Toby Conglomerate comprises an alluvial fan sequence whose grain-size distribution, paleocurrents and present-day morphological exposure parallel the exposed geometry of an alluvial fan deposit (Figure 8). Within the Mt. Toby Conglomerate, vertical sequences, as discussed in the preceding section, are common. The Devonian of Norway (Nilsen, 1969) displays a complete spectrum of alluvial fan facies (Figure 7).

BRAIDED STREAMS

Braided streams refer to those which show a bifurcating and anastomosing channel pattern (Figure 9) and they are common to terrains of moderate slope and moderate to low discharge. These streams owe their origin to fluctuations in flow velocity which cause transported sediment to be deposited as a series of bars (braid bars) within a channel system. Subsequent flow and reworking extends the pattern in a downstream direction. This pattern also develops in response to the high stream width to depth ratio.

The flow patterns of braided streams are uni-directional. A discussion of the velocity spectrum and flow patterns is covered in Leopold et al (1964), Rust (1972), Williams and Rust (1969) and Smith (1970, 1971). Doeglas (1962) presented a classic study of the sandy braided Durance River in France, which has served as a reference for European sedimentologists, but his paper lacks details about the exact nature of flow processes and sedimentary responses.

Braided Stream Processes and Sediments

Braided streams tend to form on surfaces of moderate to high slope and develop longitudinal bars within its channels. As the bar builds vertically above stream level, the channel splits and bifurcates. Flow instability caused by such bar development enhances nonuniform flow velocity which localizes deposition of additional bars. Bar development causes coarse sediment shields to accumulate on the up-current end of individual bars, whereas sand and silt are deposited in the longitudinal direction of the bar (Williams and Rust, 1969; Rust, 1972; Williams, 1971). The longitudinal bars are characterized by cross-strata (Williams, 1971) and decrease in particle size downstream. Within the braided stream system, as demonstrated by Smith (1971) from the Lower Platte River of Nebraska, transverse bars are also known to develop (Figure 10). Their development tends to occur dominantly during relatively low discharge and low water level phases when cross-channel flow patterns are known. Under such conditions, braid bars are cut by newly-formed channels which transported sediment into deeper portions of existing channels as a barlike form. Bar progradation in such a localized flow direction maintains and expands the bar (Figure 10). Bar build-up and development is rapid; Smith (1971) reported the total life span of Lower Platte River bars to be on the order of four to five days. The bars contain parallel laminae (Rust, 1972; Smith, 1971), cross-stratification (Smith, 1971; Williams, 1971) and ripple bedforms (Figure 11).

Sedimentary Structures.

The sedimentary structures within braided streams are highly variable consisting of both upper flow regime and lower flow regime types. Parallel laminae are most common to longitudinal and transverse bars as are both accretionary and avalanche cross-stratification. This cross-stratification develops, as Smith (1971) pointed out, by a process analogous to growth of laboratory deltas (See Joplin, 1966). Within the channels, the style of stratification can more commonly be described as "cut-and-fill" and includes trough-shaped truncated cross-strata, some with clayey drapes associated with local troughs which are abandoned temporarily. Current ripples normally occur on the surfaces of bars.

Vertical Sequence.

The vertical sequence of sedimentary structures, grain size and lithology of braided streams has only been adequately documented in one case. Costello and Walker (1972) described some Pleistocene sediments in southern Ontario which they interpret to represent proglacial outwash braided stream deposits. These sediments are dominantly sand gravels, and within the braided channel fills only, several coarsening-upward sequences were documented (Figure 12). These sequences start with a basal clay representing initial overbank deposition into an abandoned channel, and are overlain by silts and sands with cross-strata deposited during a subsequent flooding event. As the major channel system shifted into is prior position, coarser, cross-stratified sands and gravels were deposited, following which levee breaching occurred and a capping sequence of thicker sets of cross-stratified sandy gravel was deposited.

Ancient Examples

Braided stream deposits have been identified in very few ancient examples. Perhaps the most convincing cases occur in the Triassic of Novia Scotia (Klein, 1962), and the Tuscarora Sandstone of Pennsylvania (Smith, 1970). More recently, Voss (1975) re-examined and reviewed the existing data concerning the placer gold-bearing sedimentary rocks of the Precambrian Witwatersrand Basin of

South Africa. There, gold-bearing sedimentary rocks define paleochannel trends (Figure 13). These sedimentary rocks are characterized by both coarsening-upward sequences and fining-upward sequences. Vos (1975) considers both to represent braided conditions, and suggests that the fining-upward sequences comprise part of a lower braided alluvial plain (deposited on a lower sloping surface) and the coarsening-upward sequences comprise part of an upper alluvial plain (higher slope angle). These lateral facies (Figure 14) develop as coarsening-upward sequences of the upper braided plain prograded basinward over the lower braided plain facies, with fining-upward successions.

MEANDERING STREAMS

Sedimentologically, the meandering alluvial valley model is the best documented of the three alluvial models reviewed herein. The data base for this model comes from studies of the Lower Mississippi River by Fisk (1944, 1947), the Red River (Harms MacKenzie, and McCubbin, 1963, the Brazos River (Bernard et al, 1962, 1970) and more recently, the River Endrick in Scotland (Bluck, 1971), and the Lower Wabash River of Illinois (Jackson, 1973, 1975a, 1975b).

Flow Processes

The hydraulics of meandering flow systems has been reviewed extensively by Leopold et al. (1964) and Allen (1965) and developed further in two forthcoming papers by Jackson (1975a, 1975b). Essentially, the meandering form superimposes on the flow system a nonuniform velocity pattern (Figure 15). Higher velocities of flow are confined to the thalweg or deeper portion of the channel, and lower velocities appear to be more characteristic of point bar zones. This general model, as Jackson (1975a, 1975b) shows is more complicated and controls the distribution of bedforms, facies and grain size distributions.

The flow velocity changes, in a down-stream direction, from high to low and back to high, as a reference flow line passes through a deeper thalweg, over a point bar and through the next thalweg downstream. As a consequence, the linear path of sediment transport tends to follow the flow lines of stream channel flow, rather than crossing back and forth. This manner of sediment transport was documented experimentally by Friedkin (1945). One of the consequences of such flow systems as stressed particularly by Jackson (1975a, b) and also by Bluck (1971), is that point bars build by elongation in a downstream direction as an enlarged longitudinal bar. Lateral cutting by the stream, however, displaces the locus of bar develop; thus lateral bar migration involves the accretion of a continuous series of longitudinal bars. Channel jumping and splitting, for flow efficiency, is also common to this setting (Fisk,1947; Allen,1965).

Meandering River Sediments and Facies

The meandering alluvial valley environment consists of a series of sedimentary facies (Figures 17 and 18) that are geomorphologically controlled. These include the main channel, which is asymmetric in section, abandoned channels, point bars, levees and flood plains. Within the channels and point bars, channel flow processes dominate. Levee build up is part of the overbank flow process and comprises the coarsest suspended load desposits. The floodplain or backswamp environment is the zone of overbank flooding and the sediment deposited there consists only of suspended load. Abandoned channels form in response to channel jumping and channel straightening.

The sediments and sedimentary facies of each of these zones is fairly well documented. The channel floor tends to consist of the coarsest debris available and consists mostly of gravels and coarse sands. The cut-bank consists of an erosional surface of pre-existing floodplain sites and clays, slump blocks of which slide into the channel floor. The lower point bar environment consists of coarse- to medium-grained cross-stratified sands, whereas the upper point bar environment tends to consist of finer-grained sands with thinner sets of cross-strata or sets of micro-cross-laminae and a surface of current ripples. The point bar facies, however, is complicated by local areas of dunes, transverse bars (generating cross-strata) and longitudinal bars which migrate laterally towards the inner bank, and generate a set of cross-strata oriented nearly at right angles to the flow directions of the river system. In some regions, coarser sediment distributions changes these relations slightly as demonstrated by Bluck (1971) from the River Endrick of Scotland (Figures 16 and 19).

Vertical Sequences

The dominant mode of lateral sedimentation generates a fining-upward vertical sequence (Nanz, 1954; Bersier,

1958; Bernard et al, 1962, 1970; Allen, 1963; Visher, 1965, 1972) which is summarized in Figure 20 and 21. This fining-upward sequence starts with a basal scour overlain by a lag concentrate of channel bottom gravels. These are overlain by coarse sands which are parallel laminated or cross-bedded, representing the earliest channel fill. Overlying these sediments are the lower point bar finer sands which are thinner-bedded and micro-cross-laminated. The top of the sequence consists of overbank silts and clays from the levee and gloodplain environment.

This sequence has been documented from many ancient examples also (Figures 22, 23, 24) and in turn controls the characteristics of electric log patterns as shown by Bernard et al. (1970), Harms (1966) and MacKenzie (1972; See also Figures 25, 26, and 27). They serve as an important clue to environmental identification in subsurface geological studies.

Ancient Examples of Meandering Stream Deposits.

Allen (1965) has compiled several ancient examples of meandering streams, and several more have been documented since. Allen's (1964, 1965) classic study of the Devonian Old Red Sandstone of England (Figure 22) is one of the best-documented cases. However, Belt (1968) and Stanley (1968) have documented similar deposits, including a crevasse-splay sequence from the Carboniferous of Nova Scotia and Massachusetts, respectively (Figures 23, 24). Ferm and Cavoroc (1968) demonstrated similar channel systems in the coal measures (Carboniferous) of West Virginia (Figure 28) and documented both meandering systems and channels characterized by a history of channel jumping. In all these studies, the documentation of fining-upward sequences was the major clue to recognition of fossil meandering channel systems. Partial sequences also serve as a clue, and in one case, paleohydraulic variables were determined from a Cretaceous example (Cotter, 1971). The above examples are just a partial list of ancient examples. The Cretaceous of the Gulf Coastal Plain (Pryor, 1961) and of the Rocky Mountains (Masters, 1967) contain many examples of meandering stream systems.

OIL FIELD EXAMPLES OF FLUVIAL SEDIMENTS.

The best oil field examples appear to occur only in sedimentary rocks that were formed by meandering streams in preserved coastal plain settings of low relief. The first

such oil field example to be so documented are the Frio
trends (Oligocene) of southern Texas (Nanz, 1954). There
oil occurrences are closely related to meandering channel
systems documented from fining-upward sequences.

Harms (1966) and MacKenzie (1972) have documented
several stratigraphic traps from the Cretaceous of the
Rocky Mountains. There, fining-upward sequences could be
recognized, as could the sinuous meandering channel pattern
from isopachous mapping. The electric log characterisitics
of these sandstones (Figures 26 and 27) show a high
self-potential and higher resistivity in the lower coarser
zone, with a sharp demarkation with respect to underlying
mudstones. The values of the SP and Resistivity reduce
upward; these properties are controlled, of course, by the
fining-upward nature of the sandstone beds deposited by
laterally-migrating meandering streams.

These features of meandering channels also are
distinct in their seismic nature as shown by Harms and
Tackenberg (1972; See Figure 29).

URANIUM OCCURENCES.

The fluvial channel bottom environment appears
also to be a favorable occurrence for sandstone-type
uranium ores, particularly in the Morrisson Formation of
the Colorado Plateau (Schlee and Moench, 1961) and along
the Gulf Coastal Plain (Eargle et al, 1975). In the Gulf
Coastal Plain, uranium mineralization is confined to
channels (Figure 30). The origin of these ores has been
controversial and a discussion is beyond the scope of this
syllabus. However, the following possibilities are to be
considered:

(1)   Uranium is coprecipitated by organic-rich
        lag concentrates in channel bottoms.

(2)   Uranium is transported detritally and
        concentrates as a placer.

(3)   Uranium minerals are a diagenetic byproduct
        of ground-water flow and alteration of
        unstable iron-uranium minerals are
        concentrated diagenetically (Walker, 1975).
        This process is not unlike the insitu
        alteration of iron-bearing minerals which
        form redbeds (Walker, 1967, 1974).

Each of these modes of formation are tied to fluvial systems draining areas of moderate to high relief with granitic and metamorphic terrains which acted as uranium sources.

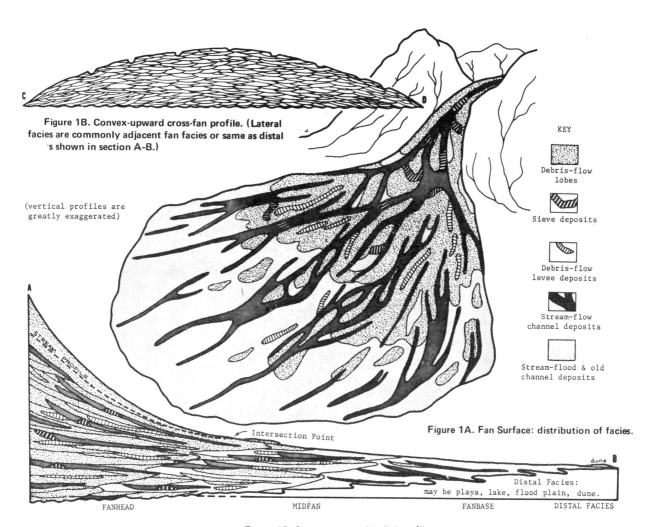

Figure 1B. Convex-upward cross-fan profile. (Lateral facies are commonly adjacent fan facies or same as distal 's shown in section A-B.)

(vertical profiles are greatly exaggerated)

KEY

Debris-flow lobes

Sieve deposits

Debris-flow levee deposits

Stream-flow channel deposits

Stream-flood & old channel deposits

Figure 1A. Fan Surface: distribution of facies.

Intersection Point

Distal Facies: may be playa, lake, flood plain, dune.

FANHEAD   MIDFAN   FANBASE   DISTAL FACIES

Figure 1C. Concave-upward radial profile.

FIGURE 1. Distribution of sediment facies and morphological profiles of an ideal alluvial fan (From Spearing, 1975; Reprinted by permission of the Geological Society of America)

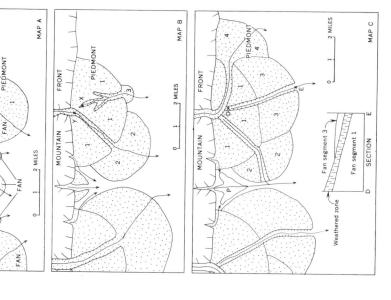

FIGURE 3. Development of alluvial fan from initial state (A), to entrenched stage with build-up of new fan (B) to final stage leading to formation of bajada (From Denny, 1967).

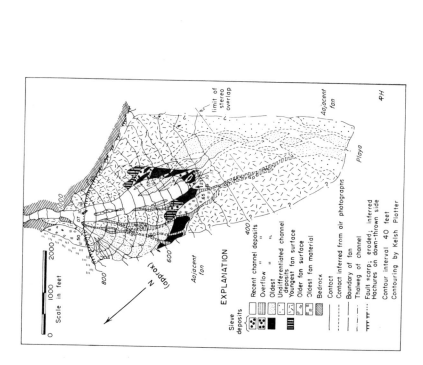

FIGURE 2. Geomorphic map of the Shadow Rock Fan, California (from Hooke, 1967; reprinted by permission of the University of Chicago Press).

14

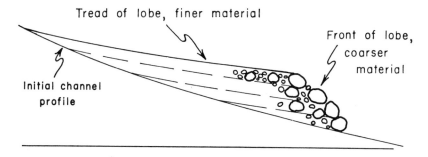

FIGURE 4. Model for growth of sieve lobe on alluvial fan (from Hooke, 1967; reprinted by permission of the University of Chicago Press).

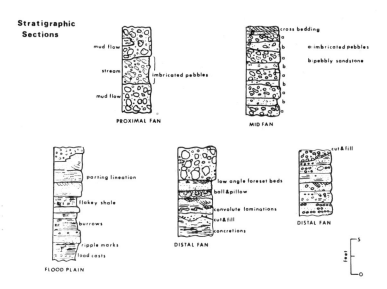

FIGURE 5. Vertical sequences within alluvial fan facies, Triassic, Massachusetts (From Wessel, 1969; reprinted by permission of the Dept. of Geology, University of Massachusetts).

15

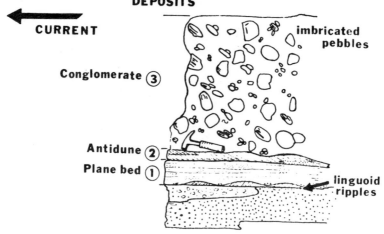

FIGURE 6. Upper flow regime sedimentary sequence in Triassic alluvial fan (From Wessell, 1969; Reprinted by permission of the Dept. of Geology, Univ. of Massachusetts).

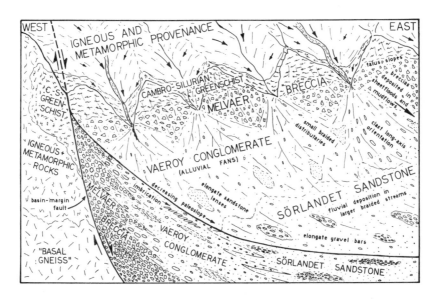

FIGURE 7. Devonian depositional environments, Buelandet-Vaerlandet region, Norway (From Nilsen, 1969).

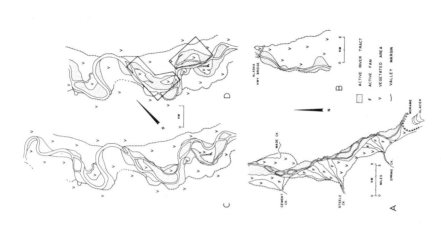

FIGURE 9. Variability of braided drainage patterns, Donjek River Valley, Yukon, Canada (From Rust, 1972).

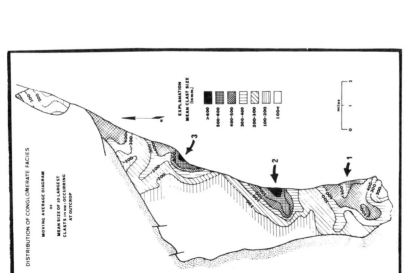

FIGURE 8. Moving averages of mean size of ten largest clasts defining alluvial fan complexes, Triassic, Massachusetts (From Wessell, 1969; reprinted by permission of the Dept. of Geology, University of Massachusetts).

FIGURE 10. Maps showing changes in shape, flow characteristics and bedform distribution for a single transverse bar, Platte River, Nebraska, over a five-day period. (From Smith, 1971; reprinted by permission of the Geological Society of America).

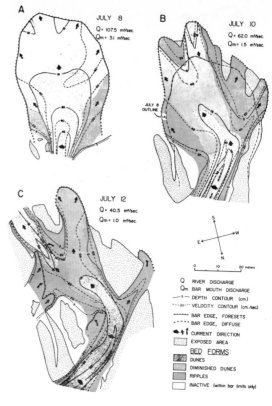

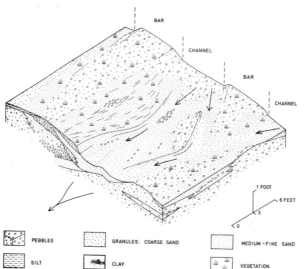

FIGURE 11. Three-dimensional model of braided bar facies (From Williams and Rust, 1969; Reprinted by permission of the Society of Economic Paleontologists and Mineralogists).

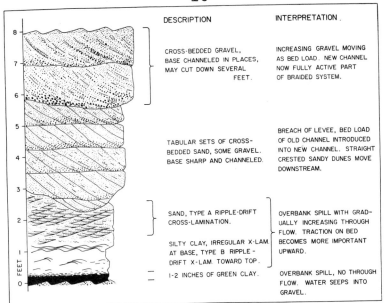

Coarsening-upward sequence, braided Pleistocene sediments, Credit River, Ontario (From Costello and Walker, 1972; Reprinted by permission of the Society of Economic Paleontologists and Mineralogists).

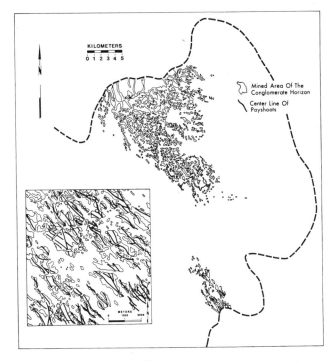

FIGURE 13. East Rand, South Africa, showing mined conglomerate horizons which define braided stream pattern and which also delineate gold pay-shoot zones (From Vos, 1975; Reprinted by permission of the Society of Economic Paleontologists and Mineralogists).

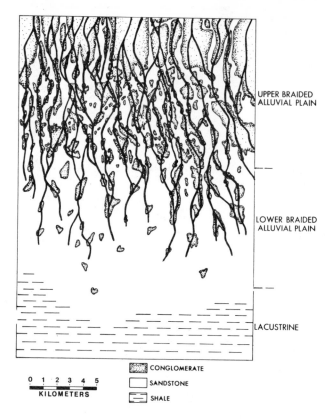

FIGURE 14. East Rand district, South Africa showing paleogeographic map of Precambrian gold-bearing braided stream deposits (From Vos, 1975; reprinted by permission of the Society of Economic Paleontologists and Mineralogists).

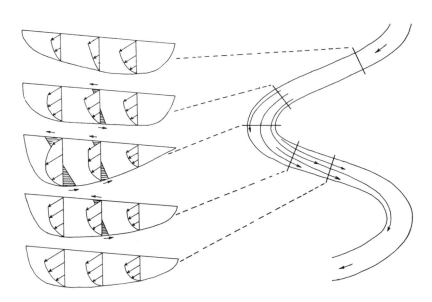

FIGURE 15. Flow pattern in a meandering river channel (From Allen, 1965; after Leopold et al., 1964).

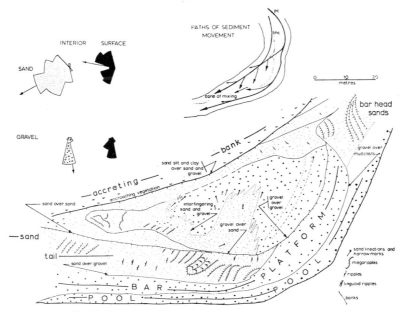

FIGURE 16. Bar head of typical point bar, River Endrick, Scotland, showing direction of sediment movement, and orientation of surface and internal directional structures (From Bluck, 1971).

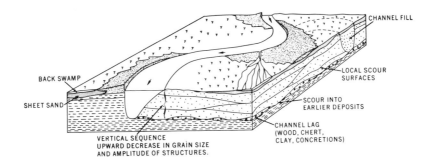

FIGURE 17. Meandering alluvial valley depositional model after Visher (1972; Reprinted by permission of the Society of Economic Paleontologists and Mineralogists).

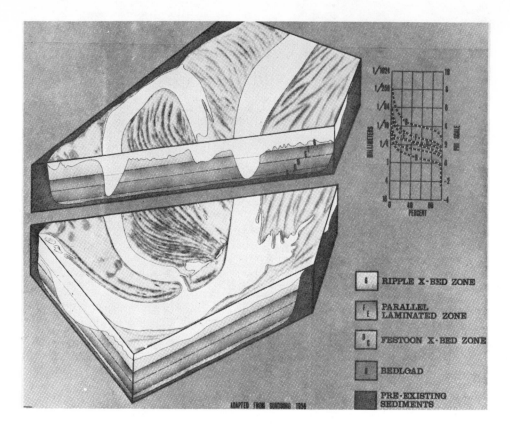

FIGURE 18. Distribution of structures and grain size, River Klaralven, Sweden (From Visher, 1972; after Sundborg, 1956; Reprinted by permission of the Society of Economic Paleontologists and Mineralogists).

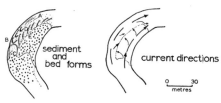

FIGURE 19. Sedimentary sequence at bar head in River Endrick, Scotland, meandering point bar (From Bluck, 1971).

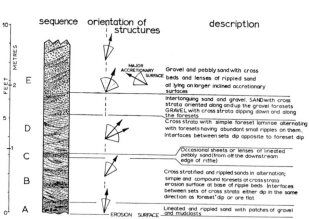

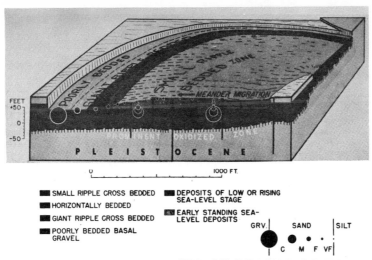

POINT BAR DEPOSITS OF BRAZOS RIVER

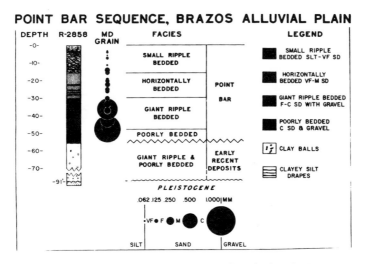

FIGURE 20. Depositional sequence on Blasdel Point Bar, Brazos River, Texas (From Bernard et al., 1970; reprinted by permission of the Texas Bureau of Economic Geology).

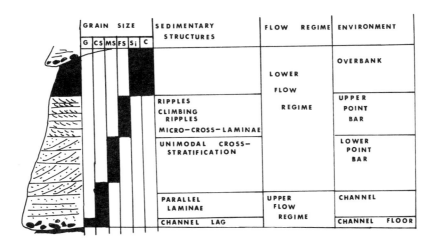

FIGURE 21. Generalized fining-upward meandering alluvial valley model (From Klein, 1972; Reprinted by permission of the Geological Society of America).

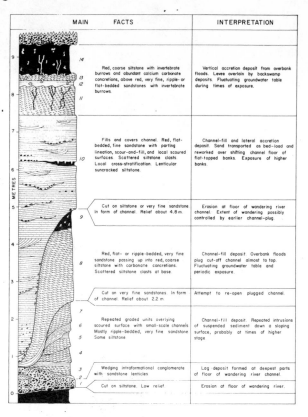

FIGURE 22. Fining-upward sequence, Old Red Sandstone (Devonian), Tugford, Anglo-Welsh Borderland, UK (From Allen, 1965).

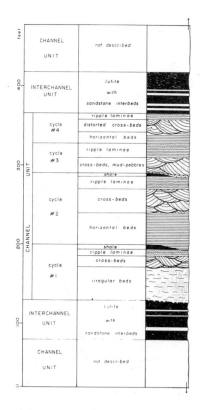

FIGURE 23. Vertical sequences of primary structures and lithologies subdivided into channel units, Ross Point Formation (Carboniferous), Alma, New Brunswick (From Belt, 1968; Reprinted by permission of the Geological Society of America.)

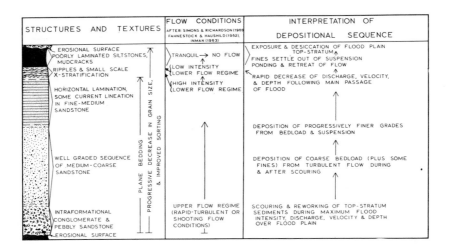

STRUCTURES AND TEXTURES	FLOW CONDITIONS AFTER: SIMONS & RICHARDSON (1961) FAHNESTOCK & HAUSHILD (1962), INMAN (1963)	INTERPRETATION OF DEPOSITIONAL SEQUENCE
EROSIONAL SURFACE POORLY LAMINATED SILTSTONES, MUDCRACKS	TRANQUIL → NO FLOW LOW INTENSITY LOWER FLOW REGIME HIGH INTENSITY LOWER FLOW REGIME	EXPOSURE & DESICCATION OF FLOOD PLAIN TOP-STRATUM FINES SETTLE OUT OF SUSPENSION PONDING & RETREAT OF FLOW RAPID DECREASE OF DISCHARGE, VELOCITY, & DEPTH FOLLOWING MAIN PASSAGE OF FLOOD
RIPPLES & SMALL SCALE X-STRATIFICATION		
HORIZONTAL LAMINATION, SOME CURRENT LINEATION IN FINE-MEDIUM SANDSTONE		DEPOSITION OF PROGRESSIVELY FINER GRADES FROM BEDLOAD & SUSPENSION
WELL GRADED SEQUENCE OF MEDIUM-COARSE SANDSTONE		DEPOSITION OF COARSE BEDLOAD (PLUS SOME FINES) FROM TURBULENT FLOW DURING & AFTER SCOURING
INTRAFORMATIONAL CONGLOMERATE & PEBBLY SANDSTONE EROSIONAL SURFACE	UPPER FLOW REGIME (RAPID-TURBULENT OR SHOOTING FLOW CONDITIONS)	SCOURING & REWORKING OF TOP-STRATUM SEDIMENTS DURING MAXIMUM FLOOD INTENSITY, DISCHARGE, VELOCITY & DEPTH OVER FLOOD PLAIN

FIGURE 24. Fining-upward sequence in Pennsylvania Wamsutta Formation, Massachusetts, showing also interpreted flow conditions and depositional events (From Stanley, 1968; Reprinted by permission of the Geological Society of America).

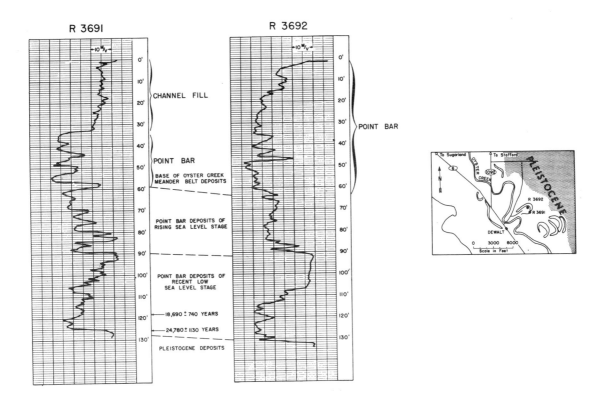

FIGURE 25. SP logs of channel fill and point bar deposits, Holocene Brazos River showing control of vertical sequence on SP properties (From Bernard et al., 1970; Reprinted by permission of the Texas Bureau of Economic Geology).

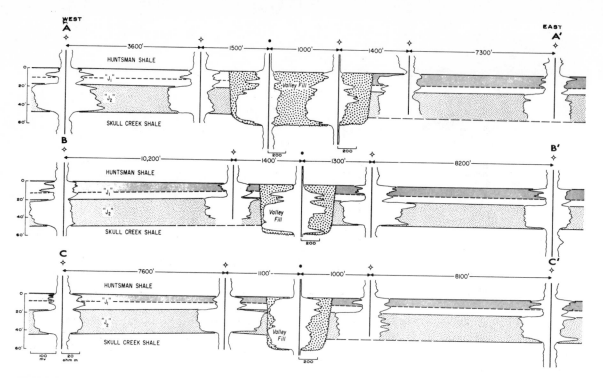

FIGURE 26. Electric-log cross-sections showing valley fill stratigraphic trap, "J" Sandstone (Cretacious), Nebraska. Shape of SP and resistivity curves tends to reflect fining-upward nature of valley fill (From Harms, 1966; reprinted by permission of the American Association of Petroleum Geologists).

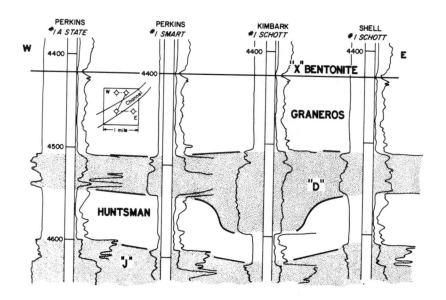

FIGURE 27. Electric log cross-section of "D" Sandstone (Cretaceous), Logan County, Colorado, showing how fining-upward sequence controls SP and resistivity characteristics (From MacKenzie, 1972; Reprinted by permission of the American Association of Petroleum Geologists).

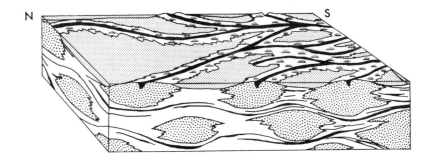

FIGURE 28. Generalized litho-genetic model for fluvial and other non-marine sediments, Carboniferous, West Virginia (From Ferm and Cavaroc, 1968; Reprinted by permission of the Geological Society of America).

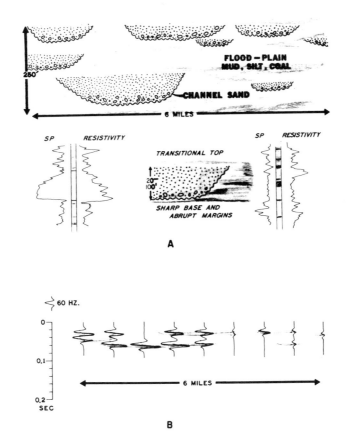

FIGURE 29. Reflectors (seismic) in stream deposits showing (A) distribution of lithologies and control of lithologic and textural properties on electric log characteristics and (B) a synthetic seismic section of A. (From Harms and Tachenberg, 1972; Reprinted by permission of the Society of Exploration Geophysicists).

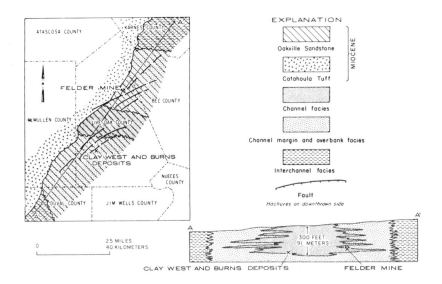

FIGURE 30. Fluvial facies in the Uraniferous Oakville Sandstone (Miocene) of Texas (From Eargle et al., 1975; Reprinted by permission of the American Association of Petroleum Geologists).

SELECTED BIBLIOGRAPHY

Allen, J.R.L., 1963, Henry Clifton Sorby and the sedimentary structures of sands and sandstones in relation to flow conditions: Geol. en. Mijnb., v. 42, p. 223-228.

_____, 1964, Studies of fluviatile sedimentation: six cyclothems from the Lower Old Red Sandstone, Anglo-Welsh basin: Sedimentology, v. 3, p. 163-198.

_____, 1965, A review of the origin and characteristics of Recent alluvial sediments: Sedimentology, v. 5, p. 88-191.

Belt, E.S., 1968, Carboniferous continental sedimentation, Atlantic Provinces, Canada, p. 127-176: in Klein, G.deV, editor, 1968, Late Paleozoic and Mesozoic continental sedimentation, northeastern North America: Geol. Soc. America Spec. Paper 106, 309 p.

Bernard, H.A., LeBlanc, R.J., and Major, C.F., 1962, Recent and Pleistocene Geology of southeast Texas: p. 175-224: in Rainwater, E.H. and Zingula, R.P., editors, 1962, Geology of the Gulf Coast and Central Texas: Houston, Houston Geol. Soc., 392 p.

Bernard, H.A., Major, C.F. Jr., Parrott, B.S. and LeBlanc, R.J., 1970,
    Brazos alluvial plain environment: Texas Bureau of Econ. Geol.
    Guidebook No. 11.

Bersier, A., 1958, Sequences detritiques et divagations fluviales: Eclog.
    Geol. Helv., v. 51, p. 854-893.

Blissenback, Erich, 1954, Geology of alluvial fans in semiarid regions:
    Geol. Soc. America Bull., v. 65, p. 175-189.

Bluck, B.J., 1965, The sedimentary history of some Triassic conglomerates
    in the Vale of Glamorgan, South Wales: Sedimentology, v. 4, p.
    225-245.

_____, 1971, Sedimentation in the meandering River Endrick, Scotland:
    Scottish Jour. Geology, v. 7, p. 93-138.

Bull., W.B., 1972, Recognition of alluvial fan deposits in the stratigraphic
    record, p. 63-83: In Rigby, J.K. and Hamblin, W.K., editors, 1972,
    Recognition of ancient sedimentary environments: Soc. Econ.
    Paleontologists and Mineralogists Spec. Pub. 16, 340 p.

Costello, W.R., and Walker, R.G., 1972, Pleistocene sedimentology, Credit
    River, southern Ontario: a new component of the braided river
    model: Jour. Sedimentary Petrology, v. 42, p. 389-400.

Cotter, Edwin, 1971, Paleoflow characteristics of a Late Cretaceous river
    in Utah from analysis of sedimentary structures in the Ferron
    Sandstone: Journ. Sedimentary Petrology, v. 41, p. 129-138.

Crowell, J.C., 1974, Sedimentation along the San Andreas Fault, California,
    p. 292-303: in Dott, R.H. Jr., editor, 1974, Modern and Ancient
    geosynclinal sedimentation: Soc. Econ. Paleontologists and
    Mineralogists Spec. Pub. 19, 380 p.

Denny, C.S., 1967, Fans and pediments: Am. Jour. Sci., v. 265, p. 81-105.

Doeglas, D.J., 1962, The structure of sedimentary deposits in braided
    rivers: Sedimentology, v. 1, p. 167-190.

Eargle, D.H., Dickinson, K.A., and Davis, B.A., 1975, South Texas Ura-
    nium deposits: Am. Assoc. Petroleum Geologists Bull., v. 59, p. 766-779.

Ferm, J.C., and Cavaroc, V.V. Jr., 1968, A nonmarine sedimentary model
    for the Allegheny rocks of West Virginia, p. 1-20: in Klein,
    G.deV., editor, 1968, Late Paleozoic and Mesozoic continental
    sedimentation, northeastern North America: Geol. Soc. America
    Spec. Paper 106, 309 p.

Fisk, H.N., 1944, Geological investigation of the alluvial valley of the
    Lower Mississippi River: Vicksburg, Mississippi River Commission,
    78 p.

_____, 1947, Fine-grained alluvial deposits and their effect on Mississippi River activity: Vicksburg, Mississippi River Commission, 82 p.

Friedkin, J.F., 1945, A laboratory study of the meandering of alluvial rivers: Visckburg, Mississippi River Commission, 40 p.

Hand, B.M., Hayes, M.O., and Wessell, J.M., 1969, Antidunes in the Mount Toby Formation (Triassic), Massachusetts: Jour. Sedimentary Petrology, v. 39, p. 1310-1316.

Harms, J.C., 1966, Stratigraphic traps in a valley fill, western Nebraska: Am. Assoc. Petroleum Geologists Bull., v. 50, p. 2119-2149.

Harms, J.C., MacKenzie, D.B. and McCubbin, D.G., 1963, Stratification in modern sands of the Red River, Louisiana: Jour. Geology, v. 71, p. 556-580.

Harms, J.C. and Tachenberg, P., 1972, Seismic signatures of sedimentation models: Geophysics, v. 37, p. 45-58.

Hooke, R.L., 1967, Processes on arid-region alluvial fans: Jour. Geology, v. 75, p. 438-460.

Jackson, R.G., II, 1973, Velocity-bedform-tecture pattern of meander bends in the Lower Wabash River (Abs): Geol. Soc. America Abs. with Programs, v. 5, p. 681.

_____, 1975a, Hierarchial attributes and a unifying model of bedforms composed of cohesionless material and produced by shearing flow: Geol. Soc. America Bull., v. 86 (In Press).

_____, 1975b, Velocity-bedform-texture patterns of meander bends in the Lower Wabash River: Geol. Soc. America Bull., v. 86, (In Press).

Joplin, A.V., 1966, Some applications of theory and experiment to the study of bedding genesis: Sedimentology, v. 7, p. 71-102.

Klein, G.deV., 1962, Triassic sedimentation, Maritime Provinces, Canada: Geol. Soc. America Bull., v. 73, p. 1127-1146.

_____, 1972, Sedimentary model for determining paleotidal range: reply: Geol. Soc. America Bull., v. 83, p. 539-546.

Leopold, L.B., Wolman, M.G., and Miller, J.P., 1964, Fluvial processes in geomorphology: San Francisco, W.H. Freeman & Co., 522 p.

MacKenzie, D.B., 1972, Primary stratigraphic traps in sandstones, p. 47-63: in Stratigraphic Oil and Gass Fields: Am. Assoc. Petroleum Geologists Memoir 16.

Masters, C.D., 1967, Use of sedimentary structures in determination
        of depositional environments, Mesaverde Formation, Willaims Fork
        Mountains, Colorado: Am. Assoc. Petroleum Geologists Bull., v. 51,
        p. 2033-2043.

Nanz, R.H., Jr., 1954, Genesis of Oligocene sandstone reservoir,
        Seeligso Field, Jim Wells and Kleberg Counties, Texas: Am.
        Assoc. Petroleum Geologists Bull., v. 38, p. 96-117.

Nilsen, T.H., 1969, Old Red sedimentation in Buelander-Vaerlandet
        Devonian district, western Norway: Sed. Geology., v. 3, p. 35-57.

Pryor, W.A., 1961, Sand trends and paleoslope in Illinois Basin and
        Mississippi Embayment, p. 119-133: in Peterson, J.A. and Osmond,
        J.C., editors, 1961, Geometry of sandstone bodies: Am. Assoc.
        Petroleum Geologists, 240 p.

Rust, B.R., 1972, Structures and process in a braided river: Sedi-
        mentology, v. 18, p. 1171-1178.

Schlee, J.S. and Moench, R.H., 1961, Properties and genesis of
        "Jackpile" Sandstone, Laguna, New Mexico, p. 134-150: in
        Peterson, J.A. and Osmond, J.C., editors, 1961, Geometry of
        sandstone bodies: Tulsa, Am. Assoc. Petroleum Geologists, 240 p.

Smith, N.D., 1970, The braided stream depositional environment: com-
        parison of the Platte River with some Silurian clastic rocks,
        north-central Appalachians: Geol. Soc. America Bull., v. 81, p. 2993-3014.

_____, 1971, Transverse bars and braiding in the Lower Platte
        River, Nebraska: Geol. Soc. America Bull., v. 82, p. 3407-3420.

Spearing, D.R., 1975, Summary sheets of sedimentary deposits: Geol.
        Soc. America Publication MC-8.

Stanley, D.J., 1968, Graded bedding-solemarking-graywacke assemblage
        and related sedimentary structures in some Carboniferous flood
        deposits, eastern Massachusetts, p. 211-240: in Klein, G.deV,
        editor, 1968, Late Paleozoic and Mesozoic continental
        sedimentation, northeastern North America: Geol. Soc. America
        Spec. Paper 106, 309 p.

Sundborg, Ake, 1956, The River Klaralven: Geog. Annaler, v. 38,
        p. 127-316.

Visher, G.S., 1965, Use of the vertical profile in environmental
        reconstruction: Am. Assoc. Petroleum Geologists Bull., v. 49, p. 41-61.

_____, 1972, Physical characteristics of fluvial deposits, p. 84-
        97: in Rigby, J.K. and Hamblin, W.K., editors, 1972, Recognition
        of ancient sedimentary environments: Soc. Econ. Paleontologists
        and Mineralogists Spec. Pub. 16, 340 p.

Vos, R.G., 1975, An alluvial plain and lacustrine model for the Precambrian Witwatersrand deposits of South Africa: Journ. Sedimentary Petrology, v. 45, p. 480-493.

Walker, T.R., 1967, Formation of red beds in modern and ancient deserts: Geol. Soc. America Bull., p. 78, p. 353-368.

_____, 1975, Intrastratal sources of Uranium in first-cycle, nonmarine red beds (Abs): Am. Assoc. Petroleum Geologists Bull., v. 59, p. 925.

Wessell, J.M., 1969, Sedimentary history of upper Triassic alluvial fan complexes in north-central Massachusetts: Univ. of Massachusetts Dept. of Geology, Contrib. No. 2, 157 p.

Williams, G.E., 1971, Flood deposits of the sand-bed ephemeral streams of central Australia: Sedimentology, v. 17, p. 1-40.

Williams, D.F. and Rust, B.R., 1969, The sedimentology of a braided river: Jour. Sedimentary Petrology, v. 39, p. 649-679.

2

BEACH-BARRIER SAND BODIES

INTRODUCTION

Beach and barrier islands occur along <u>wave-dominated</u> coasts of low relief, or coasts which are characterized by sea cliffs of bedrock.

Studies dealing with beaches and barrier islands have had a long history going back to DeBeaumont in 1845. Some recent studies provide excellent predictive models for petroleum exploration including Bernard et al's (1962) work on Galveston Island, Texas, Van Straaten's (1965) work on the Dutch Coast, Hoyt's, Howard's and Oertel's work along the Georgia Coast, Kraft (1971) along the Delaware Coast, and Hayes (1969) study of New England beaches.

North American sedimentological thinking for developing predictive models for petroleum exploration has perhaps over-played the barrier island model. Consider the following information from Dickinson et al (1972 p. 193). Approximately 3,700 miles of the world's coastline is of the barrier type. This breaks down regionally as follows:

North America - 2,000 miles
Europe - 500 miles
South America - 400 miles
Africa - 300 miles
Asia - 300 miles
Australia - 200 miles

A great deal of caution must be used in applying this model. As North Americans, we can claim nearly 55 percent of all the world's barrier-island coastlines. In terms of total coastline, we may be dealing with perhaps less than ten percent of all of it on a world-wide basis. A compilation of tidal range data from the U.S. Department of Commerce shows that one third of world-wide coastlines are characterized by tidal ranges in excess of 6 meters. Perhaps by accident or other reasons, North America has more atidal coastlines than the rest of the world. These facts are worth pondering as we explore the value of the barrier island model for petroleum exploration.

DEPOSITIONAL PROCESSES

The major depositional processes operating on beaches and barrier islands are wind-driven wave systems. Thus the height, wave periodicity and depth of sediment scour of such waves are a function of wind velocity.

The orientation of the approach of wave fronts on the shore is also very critical in the development of beaches and barrier islands. Because most waves approach shorelines at an angle, certain portions closer to the shore will shoal. The effect of shoaling is (1) to reduce the velocity of the approaching wave front, and (2) to reorient or refract the wave front nearly parallel to the shore. Even more important is the fact that the shoaling process generates a current longshore currents and they transport sediment parallel to shore, and form spits and barrier islands. The velocity and the areal extent of longshore currents is again a function of wave velocity, wave height and wave periodicty. These processes in turn are dependent on wind velocity and the area over which wind systems drive water (fetch). Higher longshore current velocities occur during stormy periods. During storms, erosion increases, sediment transport volume increases and thus major morphological and sedimentological changes occur (Figure 31) on the beach and on the barrier island during this period. As storms dissipate, rapid sediment depositon and build up occurs. Because wind systems change seasonally, the direction of wave approach and resulting longshore current systems also changes seasonally (see Figure 36).

BEACH SEDIMENTS

Morphologically, beaches are subdivided into backshore and foreshore zones, with the foreshore sloping toward the ocean. The boundary between the foreshore and the backshore is known as the berm, and it marks the point of farthest landward erosion during storms. The foreshore zone builds up by sediment increment by the swashing and back swashing of breaking waves. Tidal coasts are characterized by foreshores consisting of ridges and runnels.

Texturally, beach sediments are generally well-sorted sands. Textural variations may, however, be a function of wave height and depth of wave scour. Thus in some New England pocket beaches, gravels are common because of extreme wave heights during winter storms.

Sedimentary structures on beaches are variable. On the foreshore, sediment deposition builds a series of low-angle accretionary cross-strata with average dip angles on the order of 8 to 10 degrees. This feature appears to be diagnostic of beaches. Other structures observed are rhombic ripples, scour marks, swash marks, cusps, shell pavements and burrows.

Within a sedimentary sequence, beaches would occur immediately above the lower shoreface zone of a coarsening-upward sequence produced due to coastline progradation.

The storm beach environment is perhaps the most variable environment on a beach. During storms, coarse sediment buildup is common to New England pocket beaches. Along the Atlantic Coastal Plain, granule gravel, shell fragments, constructional timber, refrigerator doors and other assorted manifestations of civilization (of gravel size) are dumped on the wave-cut platform on the landward side of the backshore environment. On the Oregon coast, a seasonal cycle has been documented involving spring and summer deposition of sand, winter removal of sand (depth of 2 meters) and restoration of sand during the spring.

ORIGIN OF BARRIER ISLANDS

The origin of barrier islands has been a lively and controversial topic and a large literature has grown around it. The first individual to concern himself with the problem was DeBeaumont (1845) who proposed that barrier islands developed from upbuilding of offshore bars by on-shore sediment transport of shoaling waves. Subsequent accretion to above sea level produced a barrier island. G. K. Gilbert (1885) emphasized the importance of longshore current transport which formed spits which grew to enclose off lagoons. Periodic breaching by storms and tidal action formed inlets, leaving barrier islands as a result. This model was challenged by Douglas Johnson (1919) who supported DeBeaumont categorically. Price (1962) and Otvos (1970) cited examples supporting the DeBeaumont-Johnson model.

Hoyt (1967) proposed a different model (Figure 32). He suggested that ridges developed on shore were partly submerged during post-glacial rise of sealevel. The area behind the submerged ridge became a lagoon, and the ridge was thus separated from land to become a barrier. Subsequent longshore sediment transport resulted in barrier accretion. Fisher (1968) objected to this hypothesis, and favored the Gilbert Model (Figure 33).

Along the Gulf Coastal Plain, Shepard (1963) stressed the importance of longshore currents to supply sediment, and onshore sand movement by shoaling waves to establish barriers. This model is a composite of both DeBeaumont and of Gilberg.

It is now generally agreed, as stressed by Schwartz (1971) that multiple causality of barrier island origin is the best explanation. Each of the above three models appear valid, depending on local hydrographic conditions.

The most recent model is one developed from the Georgia Coast by Jim Howard and George Oertel (personal communication), and has been covered in part already by Oertel (1972) and Oertel and Howard (1972). Their model is tied to the presence of estuaries along shore. These estuaries are flushed out during ebb tide by jet flow which build up a series of ramp shoals on the seaward side of tidal inlets separating barrier islands (Figures 34 & 35). Longshore current systems resediment the sand from these ramp shoals and accrete sand onto barrier permits further resedimentation to accrete barrier islands seaward. However, during periods when sediment discharge out of the estuaries is low, the ramp shoals undergo an erosional cycle and are destroyed. At this state, the longshore currents become erosional currents, and erode the barrier islands. Barrier building is favored during ramp shoal growth whereas erosion is favored when ramp shoals are cut off from their sediment source (Figure 37).

Subenvironments of the Barrier Island System and their Sediments

The landward side of barrier islands is comprised of a variety of environments such as inner flats, marsh, bay or lagoon. Here, swamps, mangroves and Spartina grass trap muds and silts. During storms, washover fans develop in these areas.

Coastal dunes occur on the crest of the barrier islands. Well-sorted fine-grained sands, organized into wedge-shaped sets of avalanche cross-stratification covered by wind ripples characterize this zone. These dunes are easily breached by storms.

Tidal inlets cut through barrier islands. The basal sediments in the channels are coarse gravel and shells. These are overlain by medium-grained sands which accrete over the inlet as the inlet migrates. Barrier extension involves inlet migration.

The seaward side of a barrier island consists of beaches, characterized by the features reviewed earlier in this chapter.

Barrier Island Transgressions

The best example of a transgressive barrier island system is described from the Delaware coast (Kraft 1971). Here transgression displaces barrier systems landward. Coastal retreat along Delaware shows that very little of the barrier island is preserved by transgression. In effect, wave systems associated with rising sea level "bulldoze" this sand landward, and what is left behind is a thin veneer of sand (approximately 30 cm thick). This is the well-defined "ravinement" zone discussed by Swift (1968), and it tends to be very thin when preserved at all (see Figure 40). Kraft (1971) and Swift (1968) clearly show that transgressive barrier systems have a very low preservation potential.

Barrier Island Progradation

Nearly all preserved barrier systems in the stratigraphic record owe their origin to progradation. The best example of prograding barrier islands occur along the Gulf Coast. Their development since the major still-stand of sea-level rise of about 3,500 to 5,000 BP has been documented by Bernard et al. (1962). The sediment distribution is summarized in Figure 38. Progradation generates a coarsening-upward sequence (Figure 38) which can be used to estimate water depths (Klein, 1974). The sequence consists of a basal offshore marine clay, an inner shoreface zone of interbedded muds and rippled sands, an upper shore face zone of beach sands (with common accretionary low-angle cross-stratification) with coastal sand at the top and finally overlain by back barrier lagoon or bay facies. An ancient counterpart from the Atoka Formation is shown in Figure 39, and a sedimentary log of several repeated cycles (including the intervening transgressive ravinement zone) is shown in Figure 40.

ANCIENT EXAMPLES

Barrier Islands have been recognized in several ancient sedimentary rocks, including the Cretaceous of New Mexico (Campbell, 1971), the Cretaceous of Wyoming, and the Mississippian and Silurian of the Appalachians. Some of these barriers are related to deltaic systems, whereas others are related to prograding shorelines. The Pennsylvanian-Mississipian rocks of the Black Warrior basin also contain barrier islands (Hobday, 1974).

OIL FIELD EXAMPLES

Several excellent barrier island sands have been reservoirs of hydrocarbons. Amongst the best documented ones are the Pennsylvanian "Shoestring" sands of Kansas (Sallyards and Lamont Trends), the Bisti Oil Field in New Mexico (Sabins 1962), the Deadhorse Creed Field (Wyoming), the famous Bell Creek Oil Field (Figures 41 and 42) of Montana (Berg and Davies, 1968; Davies et al., 1971) and the Cenozoic of the Niger Delta (Weber, 1971).

BEACH PROFILES

STATION HBB, HAMPTON BEACH
HAMPTON, N.H.

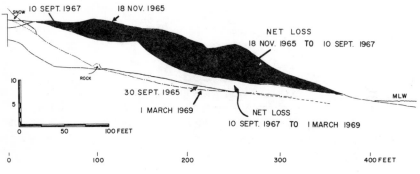

FIGURE 14-3

FIGURE 31. Changes in Beach Profile at Hampton Beach, Hampton, New Hampshire (From Hayes, 1969). Beach profile of September 1965 was changed by addition of sand by U.S. Army corps of Engineers to profile level dated November 18, 1965. Depth of storm scour and net loss up to September 19, 1967 shown by dark pattern. Stippled pattern shows additional loss up to March, 1969 (reprinted by permission of the Society of Economic Paleontologists and Mineralogists).

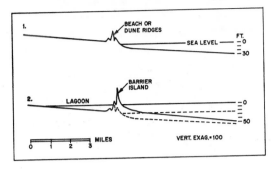

FIGURE 32. Barrier island formation by submergence (From Hoyt, 1967 and Schwartz, 1971). 1) Beach or dune ridge forms adjacent to shoreline and (2) is submerged by flooding because of sea level rise to form barrier island and lagoon (Reprinted by permission of the Geological Society of America).

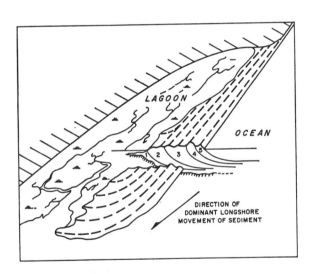

FIGURE 33. Barrier island evolution by combination of longshore current spit formation and periodic breaching by inlet formation (From Fisher, 1968 and Schwartz, 1971; after Gilbert, 1855; reprinted by permission of the Geological Society of America).

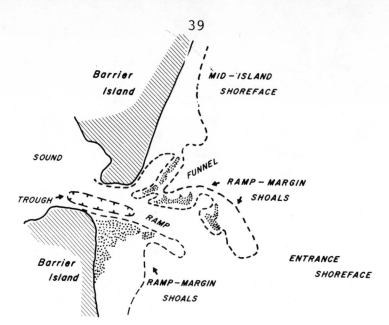

FIGURE 34. Terminology of morphological features at the barrier entrance of Georgia Coast Barrier Island system (From Oertel and Howard, 1972; Reproduced by permission from Shelf Sediment transport: Process and Pattern, edited by Donald J.P. Swift _et al_., Copyright, 1972, by Dowden, Hutchinson & Ross, Inc., Publishers, Stroudsburg, PA).

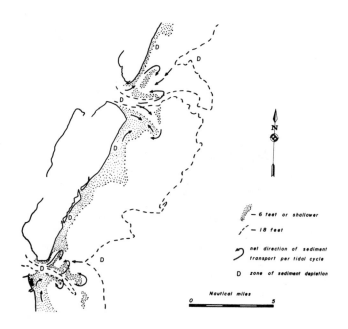

FIGURE 35. Sediment dispersal pattern in zone adjacent to depleted estuarine entrance. Sediment is trapped in closed system at entrance of estuary. Shoal progradation occurs at the expense of adjoining beaches, tidal channels and shoreface (From Oertel and Howard, 1975; Reproduced by permission from Shelf Sediment Transport: Process and Pattern, edited by Donald J.P. Swift _et al_., Copyright, 1972, by Dowden, Hutchinson & Ross, Inc., Publishers, Stroudsburg, PA).

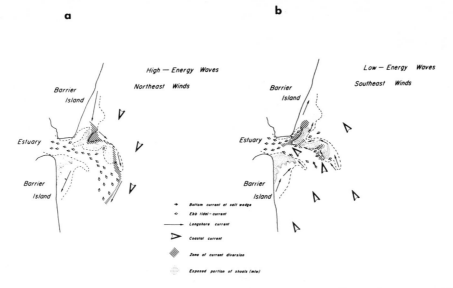

FIGURE 36. (A) Patterns of ebb-tidal currents, longshore currents and coastal currents and wave systems on Georgia estuarine entrance. Sand shifts from shoals to barriers and accretion occurs. (B) "Low-energy" pattern of ebb-tidal currents, longshore currents and coastal currents giving rise to shift in barrier build up, and re-erosion of barriers fed during northeastern storms as shown in (A) (From Oertel and Howard, 1972; Reproduced by permission from Shelf Sediment Transport: Process and Pattern, edited by Donald J.P. Swift et al. Copyright, 1972, by Dowden, Hutchinson & Ross, Inc., Publishers, Stroudsburg, PA).

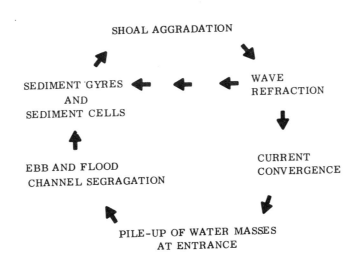

FIGURE 37. Sequence of depositional processes in development of a ramp-margin shoal. (From Oertel and Howard, 1972; Reproduced by permission from Shelf Sediment Transport: Process and pattern, edited by Donald J.P. Swift et al., Copyright, 1972, by Dowden, Hutchings & Ross, Inc., Publishers, Stroudsburg, PA).

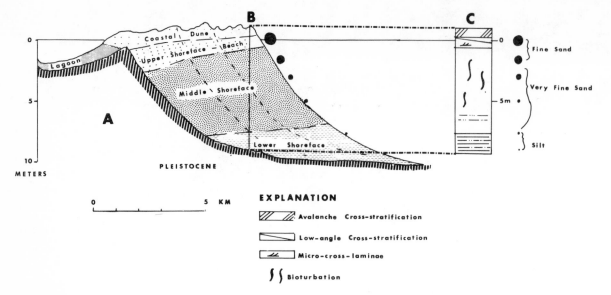

EXPLANATION

◿ Avalanche Cross-stratification

◺ Low-angle Cross-stratification

◿ Micro-cross-laminae

∫∫ Bioturbation

FIGURE 38. Vertical and lateral sediment distribution of prograding barrier island based on Galveston Island model of Bernard and others (1962). (A) Profile showing vertical and lateral sediment distribution and subenvironments. (B) Vertical section through prograded barrier island shown in Column C. (C) Vertical sequence of textures and sedimentary structures at B in prograding barrier island (From Klein, 1974; Reprinted by permission of the Geological Society of America).

FIGURE 39. Coarsening-upward sequence produced by prograding barrier island, Atoka Formation (Pennsylvanian) Winn Mountain, Arkansas.
1. Coastal dune sandstone.
2. Beach-shoreface sandstone.
3. Middle shoreface.
4. Lower shoreface mudstone.
(From Klein, 1974; Reprinted by permission of the Geological Society of America.)

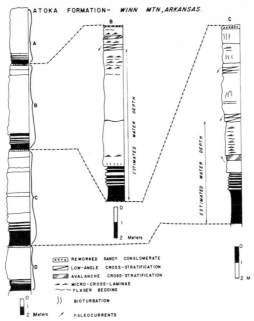

FIGURE 40. Sedimentary log showing vertical sequence of lithologies and sedimentary structures in four succeeding prograding barrier-island sequences, Atoka Formation (Pennsylvanian) Winn Mountain, Arkansas. Interval for estimating water depth as per Klein (1974) shown in expanded logs for Parts B and C. Thin ravinement zones indicated as reworked sandy conglomerate. Black-mudstone; white-sandstone (From Klein, 1974; Reprinted by permission of the Geological Society of America).

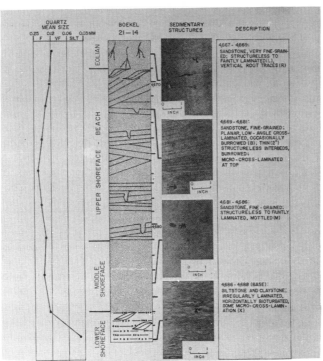

FIGURE 41. Sedimentary structures, textures and lithology of barrier island reservoir sediments, Bell Creek Field, Montana, Well 6-14 (From Davies et al., 1971; Reprinted by permission of the American Association of Petroleum Geologists).

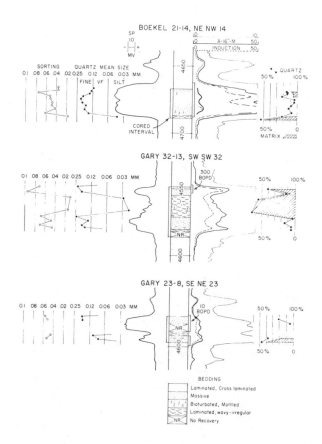

FIGURE 42. Electric log characteristics of Muddy Sandstone Facies representing barrier islands, Bell Creek Field, Montana (From Berg and Davies, 1968; reprinted by permission of the American Association of Petroleum Geologists).

SELECTED BIBLIOGRAPHY

Berg, R.R. and Davies, D.K., 1968, Origin of Lower Cretaceous Muddy
     Sandstone at Bell Creek Field, Montana: Am. Assoc. Petroleum
     Geologists Bull., v. 52, p. 1888-1898.

Bernard, H.A., LeBlanc, R.J., and Mjaor, C.F., 1962, Recent and
     Pleistocene geology of southeast Texas, field excursion no. 3
     in Geology of the Gulf Coast and Central Texas and guidebook of
     excursions: Geol. Soc. America, p. 174-224.

Campbell, C.V., 1971, Depositional model – Upper Cretaceous Gallup
     shoreline, Ship Rock area, New Mexico: Jour. Sedimentary
     Petrology, v. 41, p. 395-409.

Davies, D.K., Ethridge, F.G., and Berg, R.R., 1971, Recognition of
     barrier environments: Am. Assoc. Petroleum Geologists Bull., v. 55,
     p. 550-565.

Dickinson, K.A., Berryhill, H.L., Jr., and Holmes, C.W., 1972, Cri-
     teria for recognizing ancient barrier coastlines, p. 192-214:
     in Rigby, J.K. and Hamblin, W.K., editors, 1972, Recognition of
     ancient sedimentary environments: Soc. Econ. Paleontologists
     and Mineralogists Spec. Pub. No. 16, 340 p.

Fisher, J.J., 1968, Barrier island formation: discussion: Geol. Soc.
     America Bull., v. 79, p. 1421-1426.

Hayes, M.O., editor, 1969, Coastal environments: Northeast Massachu-
     setts and New Hampshire: Eastern Section, Soc. Econ.
     Paleontologists and Mineralogists Guidebook, 462 p.

Hobday, D.K., 1974, Beach- and barrier-island facies in the Upper
     Carboniferous of northern Alabama, p. 209-224: in Briggs,
     Garrett, 1974, Carboniferous of the southeastern United States:
     Geol. Soc. America Spec. Paper 148, 361 p.

Hoyt, J.H., 1967, Barrier island formation: Geol. Soc. America Bull,
     v. 78, p. 1125-1136.

Klein, G.deV., 1974, Estimating water depths from analysis of bar-
     rier island and deltaic sedimentary sequences: Geology, v. 2,
     p. 409-412.

Oertel, G.F., 1972, Sediment transport of estuary entrance shoals and
     the formation of swash platforms: Jour. Sedimentary Petrology,
     v. 42, p. 858-864.

Oertel, F.G., and Howard, J.D., 1972, Water circulation and sedimen-
    tation at estuary entrances on the Georgia Coast, p. 411-428:
    in Swift, D.J.P., Duane, D.B., and Pilkey, O.H., 1972, Shelf
    Sediment transport: Stroudsburg, Dowden, Hutchinson and Ross,
    656 p.

Otvos, E.G., 1970, Development and migration of barrier islands,
    northern Gulf of Mexico: Geol. Soc. America Bull., v. 81, p.
    341-348v

Sabins, F.F. Jr., 1962, How do Bisti and Dead Horse Creek strat traps
    compare: Oil and Gas Jour. for August 13, 1962, 6 p.

Schwartz, M.L., 1971, The multiple causality of barrier islands:
    Jour. Geology, v. 79, p. 91-94.

Shepard, F.P., 1963, Submarine Geology, 2nd ed: New York, Harpers,
    557 p.

Swift, D.J.P., 1968, Coastal erosion and transgressive stratigraphy:
    Jour. Geology, v. 76, p. 444-456.

Van Straaten, L.M.J.U., 1965, Coastal barrier deposits in south and
    North Holland: Meded. van Geologische Stichtung, no. 17, p. 41-75.

Weber, K.J., 1971, Sedimentological apsects of oil fields in the
    Niger Delta: Geol. en. Mijnb., v. 50, p. 559-576.

3

TIDAL FLAT AND TIDAL SAND BODIES

INTRODUCTION

The Tidal Flat zone occurs on a coastline between high and low tide levels. It is a broad plane of deposition occurring along coastlines of low relief, as well as along rocky coasts.

The best understood areas in the world are the Wadden Sea of the Netherlands, the coast of Northwest Germany, the "Wash" of the east coast of England, the Minas Basin of the Bay of Fundy of Nova Scotia, Canada, Boundary Bay, British Columbia, Canada, the north coast of Australia, and the Baja area adjoining the Colorado Delta, Mexico (see Klein, 1976 for a review).

EXAMPLES OF MODERN TIDAL FLAT SEDIMENTATION

North Sea Coast of Netherlands, Germany and England

Van Straaten, Reineck and Evans have done considerable work in these areas. Basically tidal flat environments can be subdivided into three zones--the high tidal flat, the mid flat and the low tidal flat (see Figure 42). Each of these zones is characterized by a distinct set of depositional processes and thus display contrasting and characteristic lithologies, textures and sedimentary structures which provide excellent clues for their recognition in ancient rocks. Landward from the high water mark is the supratidal zone which consists of salt marshes. Tidal channels commonly modify various tidal flat sediments.

The overall sediment distribution on tidal flats is one of seaward-coarsening. The main processes that control this seaward coarsening distribution are the length of time of submergence of the parts of the tidal flats, and the change in bottom current velocities and the bed shear during a tidal cycle (Figure 43). Seaward progradation of the tidal flat produces a typical fining-upward sequence (Figure 44).

Processes and Sediments

Low Tidal Flat: This zone is submerged for about an average of half of the tidal cycle and thus is exposed the least amount of time. Sediments in this environment are reworked by nearly the complete range of bottom velocities but mainly by bed load transport. The dominant lithology is cross-stratified sand. Current ripples, dunes and sand waves occur. Herring-bone cross-stratification is common. Both meandering channels, depositing by lateral sedimentation, and mussel banks, modify sediments in this area.

Mid-Flat: This zone is submerged for about an average of half of the tidal cycle and is subjected to alternating periods of bedload and suspension sedimentation. The main sediment type consists of interlayered thin units of sand and mud organized into flaser, lenticular and wavy bedding. Tidal bedding and current ripples occur. Meandering channels drain the mid flat environment.

High Tidal Flat: This zone is submerged for the shortest period of time coincident with the low velocity phase (slack water stage) accompanying high tide. Thus the dominant mode of deposition is by suspension. The dominant grain size is silt and clay. Clay accumulates on shore. Some burrowing is seen. Drainage channels are absent.

Supratidal--Salt Marsh Environment--This part is innundated only during spring tides. Marsh vegetation is dominant and acts as a sediment trap. The dominant sediment is clay mixed with Spartina grass. Meandering and or straight drainage channels are common.

Channels--Meandering or straight tidal channels invariably modify some parts of tidal flats. The dominant sediments are comprised of channel lag shell and mud chip gravels overlain by parallel laminae. Local fining-upward channel sequences occur.

Bay of Fundy Tidal Flats

This area is an example of tidal flat development on a rocky coast. The overall sediment distribution is seaward-coarsening, like along the Wadden Sea Coast. Wave-cut benches, estuarine clay flats, and marshes comprise additional subenvironments.

Wave Cut Benches: Seventy-five percent of the Bay of Fundy intertidal zone consists of this type of tidal flat. A thin veneer of sediment, mostly sand, covers a bedrock platform cut by tidal scour and storm waves. The sediment thickness is 10 cm.

Estuarine Clay Flats: These flats occur at the mouth of estuaries and adjoining areas. Meandering creeks traverse the silty mud zone. No channel migration is seen. The seciment color changes with depth from red at the surface to dark gray beginning at three centimeters below the surface. The clay flats provide a substrate for subsequent marsh progradation after continued vertical sediment accumulation.

Marshes: These are like the marshes from the tidal flats of the North Sea.

INTERTIDAL SAND BODIES, MINAS BASIN,
BAY OF FUNDY, NOVA SCOTIA

The Minas Basin of the Bay of Fundy is characterized by the highest tidal range in the world, making it an ideal area to study the relationship of flow dynamics of one hand, to sediment-fluid interactions and bedform evolution on the other hand. Tidal currents are characterized by time-velocity asymmetry, that is, velocities may be higher during one phase of the tidal cycle (dominant phase), than the alternating phase (subordinate). (Figure 45). In the Minas Basin, bottom current velocities reach a maximum of about 120 cm/sec. The tidal currents are completely mixed. Ebb currents generally flow westerly, whereas flood currents generally flow easterly (Figures 45 and 46).

Sediment distribution generally coarsens seaward, except for gravels along bedrock ledges and sea cliffs (Figures 47 and 48). Distribution of time-velocity asymmetry zones compares well with bar topography which is asymmetric in cross-section and linear in plan (Figures 49 and 50). Distribution of sedimentary facies is also controlled by time-velocity asymmetry zones (Figures 51 and 52) as is the orientation of dunes and sand waves (Figure 53). The features are aligned parallel to the axis of the sand body. Grain dispersal shows a radial elliptical pattern (Figure 54), but direction of maximum grain dispersal agrees with time-velocity asymmetry (Figure 54). Grain dispersal around a bar, therefore, is through alternate ebb-dominated and flood-dominated time-velocity asymmetry zones (Figure 55). Time-velocity asymmetry also produces reactivation surfaces as part of the interval anatomy of dunes and sand waves (Figure 56). These factors control sand body development in the Minas Basin region and the sand bodies are developed parallel to the dispositional strike of the basin (Figure 57.)

SUBTIDAL SAND BODIES OF TIDE-DOMINATED SHELF AREAS

Two areas in the world are known for shelves which are tide-dominated. These are the tide-dominated China Sea (flanking the Hwang Ho Delta), and the North Sea. Off and Boggs have described the China Sea sand waves and tidal sand bodies, whereas Stride, Houbolt, and Caston have described those from the North Sea of Western Europe. Off's study was primarily morphological, whereas the other papers were more sedimentologically oriented (see Klein, 1976, for a review).

In the North Sea, all the sand bodies are linear in plan, and asymmetric in section (Figure 58); they are aligned with the long axis parallel to tidal current flow (Houbolt, 1968). Sediment dispersal along the tidal sand bodies is alternatiely through ebb-dominated and flood-dominated time-velocity asymmetry zones (Figure 59). Internal anatomy is extremely complex (Figure 60). Local areas of clay deposition occur, presumably caused by periodic storm action (McCave, 1970). Data from Stride and Houbolt clearly show that the shallow subtidal sandbody of the tide-dominated shelf seas are identical to the intertidal sand bodies described from the Minas Basin of the Bay of Fundy.

ANCIENT TIDAL SAND BODIES AND TIDAL FLAT SANDSTONES

Epeiric seas like those of the Paleozoic of the Mid-continent, USA, mioclinal shelf seas of lower Paleozoic age of Nevada and Scotland, and the Cretaceous and Tertiary of the Gulf Coast are possible areas to look for ancient examples of tidal sediments. A variety of models can provide clues for the recognition and mapping of tidal sandstones in ancient rocks.

Evidence from Sedimentary Structures

A characteristic assemblage of sedimentary structures occurs in tidal sediments. This assemblage of structures can be related to various tidally controlled depositional processes (Table 1). These processes are simple reversal of tidal currents involving bedload transport, time velocity asymmetry, late stage ebb flow emergence runoff, alternation of bedload and suspension of deposition, criteria of exposure during deposition, evidences of marine life and similar other associations (see Wunderlich, 1970).

Paleocurrent Evidence

The modal pattern of paleocurrents is controlled by depositional processes. The modal data can effectively compliment sedimentary structure data. "Bipolar" and "Bimodal" orientation data fits tidal sand bodies. One of the best examples is the Eriboll Sandstone (Cambrian), discussed by Swett et al. (1971).

Textural Evidence

The textural distribution of modern tidal sediments can be related directly to tidal circulation models. This data, when associated with sedimentary structures and paleocurrent data can be used effectively for the recognition of tidal sandstones.

Tidal sands show both unimodal and bimodal distributions and are characterized by supermature rounding. Sorting and rounding are controlled by the grain dispersal model derived from the Minas Basin, Bay of Fundy (Figure 55) and from the North Sea (Houbolt, 1968) (Figure 59).

Association with Carbonate Rocks

A distinct association of tidal sandstones with shelf carbonates is seen both in the Holocene and in ancient tidal flat sediments. This criteria could provide excellent guidance to recognize ancient tidal sands.

Shinn's (1973) study of quartz grain migration in the modern Persian Gulf shows that eolian transport over carbonate sabkhas provide quartz sands to subtidal, tide-dominated zones. Thus, sabkha carbonates and associated marine carbonates, are being interbedded with quartz sands, and redeposited by tidal currents. Many ancient tidal sandstones are interbedded with intertidal carbonates. Some examples include the Zabriskie and Carrara Formations (Cambrian) of California and Nevada, the Ordovician St. Peter Sandstone--Platteville Limestone transition of Wisconsin, and the Cambrian Eriboll Sandstone--Durness Limestone of Scotland.

Paleotidal Range Model

A model is available to measure, sedimentologically, paleotidal range (Figure 42). This model shows that the thickness of the fining-upward sequence of a prograding tidal flat coincides with tidal range in Holocene settings. Fossil counterparts are known (Figure 61). Their measurement shows that ancient intertidal sediments are characterized by a paleotidal range with a fining-upward sequence (Figure 44), comparable to what would be expected with modern-day shelf seas as well as the areal extent of ancient shelf seas.

Areal Extent of Tidal Sand Bodies

The areal extent of known tidal sandstones compares very well with the areal dimension of modern shelf seas. The areal extent and size of the tide-dominated North Sea and China Sea can be used for interpreting and mapping ancient sand bodies of tidal origin.

This observation concerning areal extent fits a major principle of physical oceanography of shelf seas, namely that the wider the shelf, the higher the tidal range and associated current velocities (Redfield, 1958). Shelf width and platform width enhances tidal reworking and deposition of sand.

EXAMPLES OF TIDAL SAND PETROLEUM RESERVOIRS

A partial list includes the Cenozoic of Nigeria (Weber, 1971; see Figures 62 and 63), the Cardium Sandstone of Canada (Michaelis and Dixon, 1969), the Viking Formation of Saskatchewan, Canada (Evans, 1970), and the Permian Weislegende and Yellow Sands of western Europe (Pryor, 1970, 1971).

TABLE 1.   TIDALITE PROCESS-RESPONSE MODEL   (from Klein, 1971)

Transport Processes	Criterion
A. Tidal current bedload transport with bipolar-bimodal reversals of flow directions.	1. Cross-stratification with sharp set boundaries (Klein, 1970a) 2. Herringbone cross-stratification (Reineck, 1963) 3. Bimodal-bipolar distribution of orientation of maximum dip direction of cross-stratification (Reineck, 1963; Klein, 1967) 4. Parallel laminae (Van Straaten, 1954) 5. Complex internal organization of dunes and sand waves (Klein, 1970a; Reineck, 1963)
B. Time-velocity asymmetry of tidal current bedload transport	6. Reactivation surfaces (Klein, 1970a) 7. Bimodal or multimodal frequency distributions of set thickness of cross-strata (Klein, 1970a) 8. Bimodal frequency distribution of dip angle of cross-strata (Klein, 1970a) 9. Unimodal distribution of orientation of maximum dip direction of cross-strata (Klein, 1970a) 10. Orientation of cross-strata parallels sand body trend and basinal topographic strike (Klein, 1970a) 5. Complex internal organization of dunes and sand waves (Klein, 1970a; Reineck, 1963))
C. Late-stage emergence ebb outflow and emergence with sudden changes in flow directions at extremely shallow water depths (less than 2.0 m)	11. Trimodal distribution of orientation of maximum dip direction of cross-strata (Klein, 1970a) 12. Quadrimodal distribution of orientation of maximum dip direction of cross-strata (Evans, 1965; Klein, 1967) 13. Small current ripples superimposed at 90° or obliquely on larger current ripples (Klein, 1963, 1970; Imbrie and Buchanan, 1965) 14. Interference ripples (Reineck, 1963, 1967) 15. Double-crested current ripples (Van Straaten, 1954) 16. Flat-topped current ripples (Tanner, 1958) 17. Current ripples superimposed at 90° and 180° on crest and slip faces of dunes and sand waves, and cross-stratification (Klein, 1970a) 18. "B-C" sequences of cross-stratification overlain by micro-cross-laminae (Klein, 1970b) 19. Symmetrical ripples (Reineck, 1963) 20. Etch marks on slip faces of cross-strata (Klein, 1970a)
D. Alternation of tidal current bedload transport with suspension settlement during slack water periods	21. Cross-stratification with flasers (Reineck and Wunderlich, 1968) 22. Flaser bedding, simple (Reineck and Wunderlich, 1968) 23. Flaser bedding, bifurcated (Reineck and Wunderlich, 1968) 24. Flaser bedding, wavy (Reineck and Wunderlich, 1968) 25. Flaser bedding, bifurcated-wavy (Reineck and Wunderlich, 1968) 26. Wavy bedding (Reineck and Wunderlich, 1968) 27. Lenticular bedding, connected thick lenses (Reineck and Wunderlich, 1968) 28. Lenticular bedding, connected flat lenses (Reineck and Wunderlich, 1968) 29. Lenticular bedding, isolated thick lenses (Reineck and Wunderlich, 1968) 30. Tidal bedding (Wunderlich, 1970) 31. Convolute bedding (Dott and Howard, 1962) 32. Current ripples with muddy troughs (Reineck and Wunderlich, 1968) 33. Laminated calclutite and dololutite (Illing and others, 1965; Shinn and others, 1969)
E. Tidal slack-water mud suspension deposition	34. 22-26; 31 (from above)
F. Tidal scour	35. Mud chip conglomerates at base of washouts and channels (Reineck, 1963, 1967; Van Straaten, 1954) 36. Shell lag conglomerate at base of washouts and channels (Reineck, 1963; Klein, 1963; Van Straaten, 1952) 37. Ilots (Macar and Ek, 1965) 38. Intraformational conglomerates (Reineck, 1963, 1967) 39. Flutes (Klein, 1970a) 40. Rills (Van Straaten, 1954; Reineck, 1967)
G. Exposure and evaporation	41. Mudcracks (Van Straaten, 1954) 47. Birdseye structure (Shinn, 1968) 49. Diagenetic dolomite (Illing and others, 1965; Shinn, 1968; Deffeyes and others, 1965) 50. Nodular anhydrite (Murray, 1964) 38. Intraformation conglomerates and rip-up clasts (Reineck, 1963, 1967)
H. Burrowing and organic diagenesis	51. Depth of burrowing (Rhoads, 1967) 52. Tracks and trails (Van Straaten, 1954) 53. Drifted plant remains (Van Straaten, 1954) 54. "Impoverished fauna" (Van Straaten, 1954) 55. Laterally linked stromatolitic algal heads (Logan and others, 1964)
I. Differential compaction, loading and hydroplastic readjustment	32. Convolute bedding (Dott and Howard, 1962) 56. Load casts (Van Straaten, 1954) 57. Pseudonodules (Macar and Antun, 1950)
J. High rates of sedimentation combined with regressive sedimentation	58. Graded, fining-upward sequence (Evans, 1965; Reineck, 1963; Van Straaten and Kuenen, 1958) 59. Cyclic alternation of coarse limestone, laminated calcilutite, algal dolomite, and dololutite (Fischer, 1964)

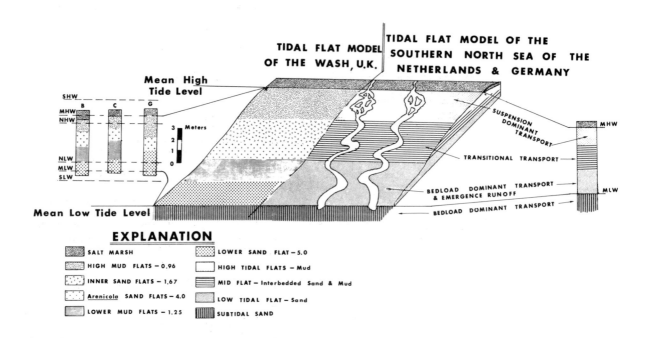

FIGURE 42. Clastic intertidal flat models for the North Sea Coast of the Wash (Evans, 1965), the Netherlands (Van Straaten, 1954) and Germany (Reineck, 1963, 1967) showing sediment distribution, sediment transport zones, vertical sequences, sand-mud ratios (numbers where pertinent) and fining upward sequences generated by prograding. Actual core logs shown for Wash. Abbreviations: SHW (Spring High Water); MHW (Mean High Water); NHW (Neap High Water); NLW (Neap Low Water); MLW (Mean Low Water); SLW (Spring Low Water); (from Klein, 1971; reprinted by permission from the Geological Society of America).

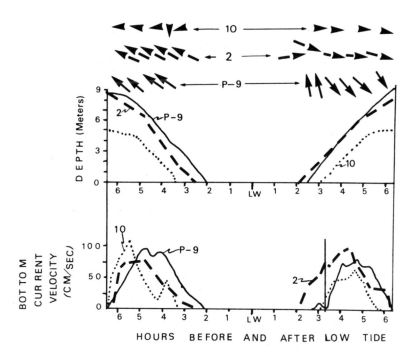

FIGURE 43. Record of 13-hour continuous observations of bottom current velocities at flood-dominated steep face of tidal sand body (Station #2), and ebb-dominated gently-sloping surfaces of Tidal sand body (Stations #10 and P-9), West Bar, Economy Point, Minas Basin, Bay of Fundy, Nova Scotia (from Klein, 1970a; reprinted by permission of the Society of Economic Paleontologists and Mineralogists).

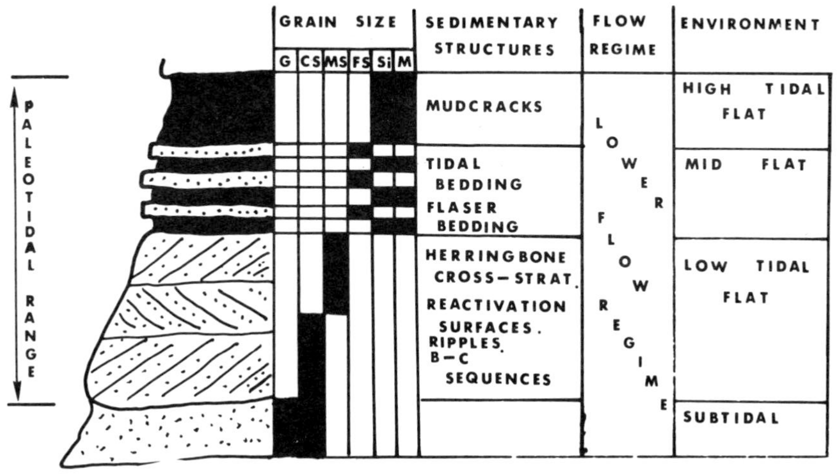

FIGURE 44. Paleotidal range fining-upward sequence (from Klein, 1972a), produced by prograding tidal flat. (Reprinted by permission of the Geological Society of America.)

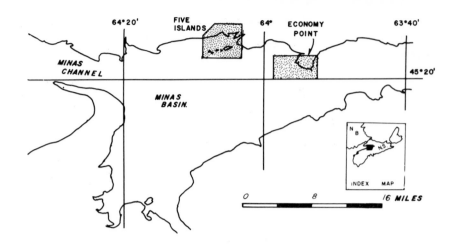

FIGURE 45. Map of Minas Basin, Bay of Fundy, Nova Scotia showing location of Five Islands and Economy Point Study areas (from Klein, 1970a; reprinted by permission of the Society of Economic Paleontologists and Mineralogists).

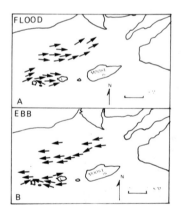

FIGURE 46. Orientation of flow directions of bottom tidal currents at Five Islands, Nova Scotia (from Klein, 1970a; reprinted by permission of the Society of Economic Paleontologists and Mineralogists).

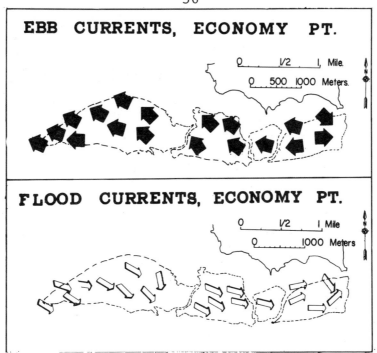

FIGURE 47. Flow directions of bottom tidal currents, Economy Point, Minas Basin Nova Scotia (from Klein, 1970a; reprinted by permission of the Society of Economic Paleontologists and Mineralogists).

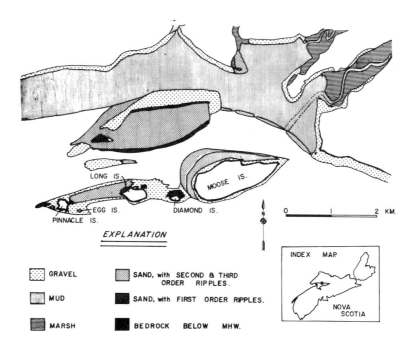

FIGURE 48. Sediment distribution map, Five Islands, Minas Basin, Nova Scotia (from Klein, 1970a; reprinted by permission of the Society of Economic Paleontologists and Mineralogists).

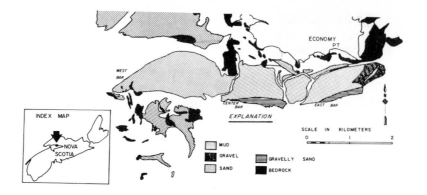

FIGURE 49: Sediment distribution, Economy Point, Minas Basin, Nova Scotia (from Klein, 1970a; reprinted by permission of the Society of Economic Paleontologists and Mineralogists).

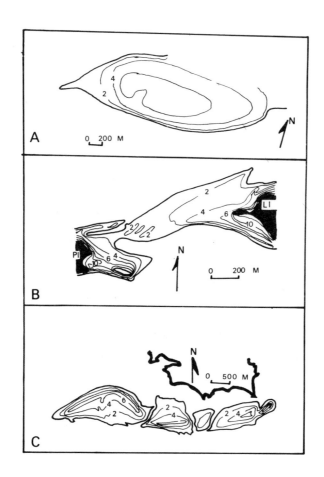

FIGURE 50: Tidal sand body topography for (A) Big Bar, Five Islands, (B) Pinnacle Flats, Five Islands, and (C) Economy Point. Contour Interval is 2 meters. Minas Basin, Bay of Fundy (from Klein, 1970a; reprinted by permission of the Society of Economic Paleontologists and Mineralogists).

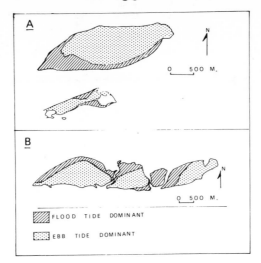

FIGURE 51: Areal distribution of time-velocity asymmetry zones for (A) Five Islands, and (B) Economy Point, Minas Basin, Bay of Fundy (from Klein, 1970a; reprinted by permission of the Society of Economic Paleontologists and Mineralogists).

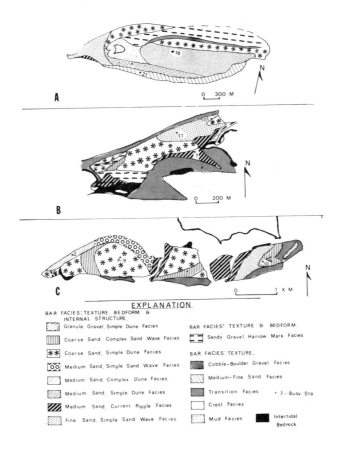

FIGURE 52: Distribution of sedimentary facies at (A) Big Bar, (B) Pinnacle Flats and (C) Economy Point, Minas Basin, Bay of Fundy, Nova Scotia (from Klein, 1970a; reprinted by permission of the Society of Economic Paleontologists and Mineralogists).

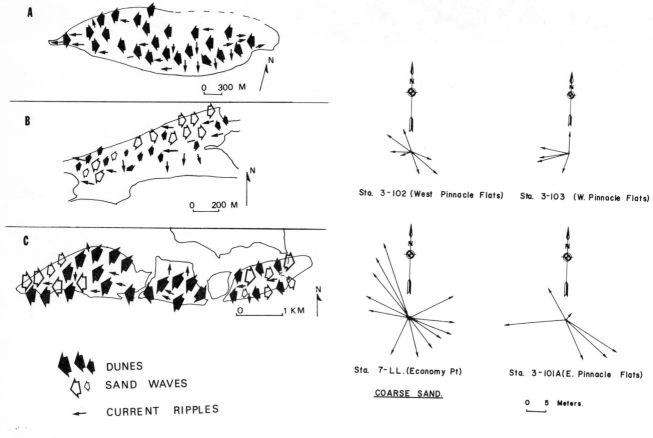

DUNES

SAND WAVES

CURRENT RIPPLES

Sta. 3-102 (West Pinnacle Flats)   Sta. 3-103 (W. Pinnacle Flats)

Sta. 7-LL.(Economy Pt)   Sta. 3-101A(E. Pinnacle Flats)

COARSE SAND.

0   5 Meters.

FIGURE 53. Orientation of bedforms at (A) Big Bar, (B) Pinnacle Flats, and (C) Economy Point, Minas Basin, Bay of Fundy, Nova Scotia (from Klein, 1970a; reprinted by permission of the Society of Economic Paleontologists and Mineralogists).

FIGURE 54. Direction of dispersal of tracer sand grains from point source, tidal sand bodies, Minas Basin, Bay of Fundy (from Klein, 1970a; reprinted by permission of the Society of Economic Paleontologists and Mineralogists.

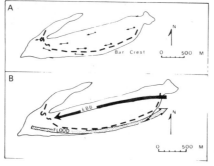

FIGURE 55. (A) Direction of maximum dispersal of sand grains from point source, after one tidal cycle at Big Bar, Pinnacle Flats. (B) Generalized sand dispersal circulation model through zones of flood and ebb-dominated tidal currents (from Klein, 1970a; reprinted by permission of the Society of Economic Paleontologists and Mineralogists.

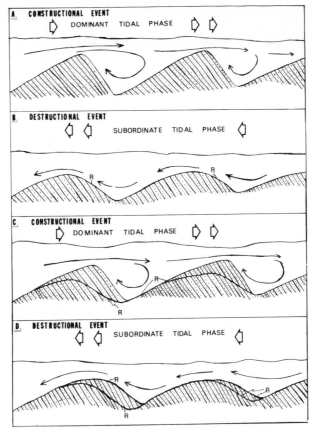

FIGURE 56. Genetic model for development of reactivation surfaces during alternation of dominant tidal phase (constructional phase) when dunes migrate, and subordinate phase (destructional event) when reactivation surfaces (R) develop. This model pertains only to areas of tidal currents characterized by time velocity asymmetry. Repeated alternation produces multiple reactivation surfaces (from Klein, 1970a; reprinted by permission of the Society of Economic Paleontologists and Mineralogists.)

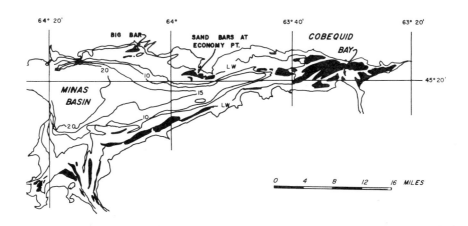

FIGURE 57. Map of Minas Basin showing bathymetry and orientation of intertidal sand bodies aligned parallel to depositional strike. Contour interval is 5 meters (from Klein, 1970a; reprinted by permission of the Society of Economic Paleontologists and Mineralogists).

FIGURE 58. Approximate isopachs of sand ridges, Well Bank, North Sea (from Houbolt, 1968; reprinted by permission of the Netherlands Geological and Mining Society).

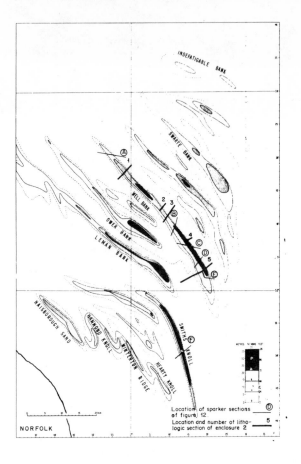

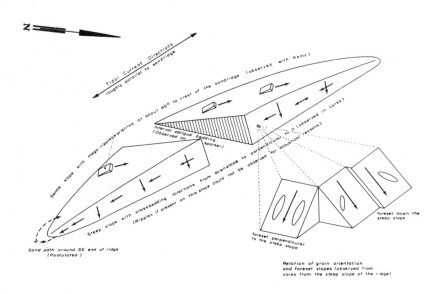

FIGURE 59. Sediment dispersal model for idealized subtidal, tide-dominated sand body, North Sea (from Houbolt, 1968; reprinted by permission of the Netherlands Geological and Mining Society).

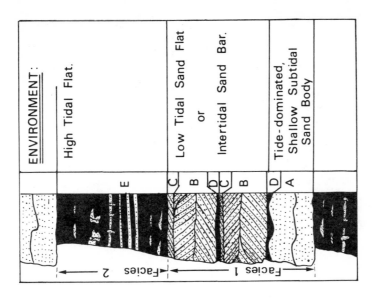

FIGURE 61. Fining-upward sequence from Precambrian tidal flat succession, Lower Fine-grained Quartzite, Islay, Scotland (from Klein, 1970b; reprinted with permission of the Society of Economic Paleontologists and Mineralogists).

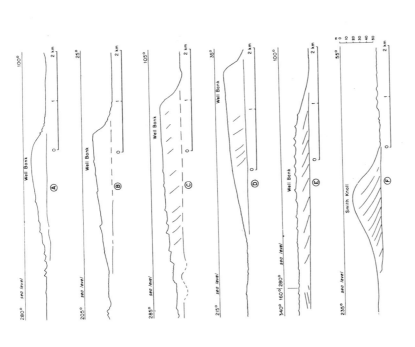

FIGURE 60. Interpretive sketch of continuous seismic profile records, Well Bank and Smith Knoll, North Sea (from Houbolt, 1968; Reprinted with permission of the Netherlands Geological and Mining Society).

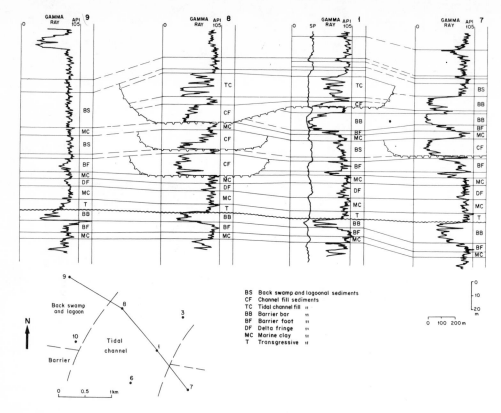

FIGURE 62. Gamma-ray log cross-section through tidal channel reservoirs, Egwa Oil Field, Nigeria (from Weber, 1971; reprinted by permission of the Netherlands Geological and Mining Society).

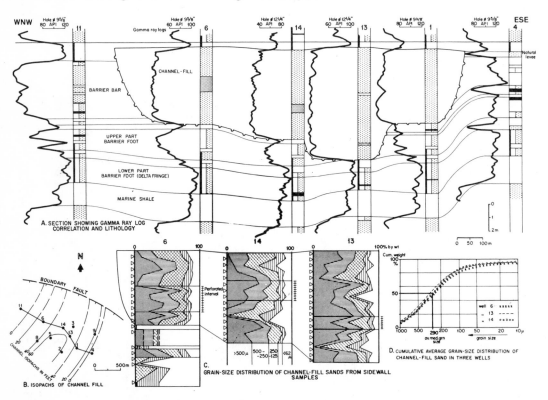

FIGURE 63. Gamma-ray log cross-section through tidal passes between barrier islands, Afierse and Eriemu Oil Fields, Nigeria (from Weber, 1971; reprinted by permission of the Netherlands Geological and Mining Society).

SELECTED BIBLIOGRAPHY

Caston, V.N.D., 1972, Linear sand banks in the southern North Sea: Sedimentology, v. 18, p. 63-78.

DeRaaf, J.F.M. and Boersma, J.R., 1971, Tidal deposits and their sedimentary structures: Geol. en. Mijnb. v. 50, p. 479-504.

Evans, Graham, 1965, Intertidal flat sediments and their environments of deposition in the Wash: Geol. Soc. London Quart, Jour., v. 121, p. 209-245.

_____, 1970, Coastal and nearshore sedimentation: a comparison of clastic and carbonate deposition: Geol. Assoc. Proc., v. 81, p. 493-508.

Evans, W.E., 1970, Imbricate linear sandstone bodies of Viking Formation in Dodsland-Hoosier area of southwestern Saskatchewan, Canada: Am. Assoc. Petroleum Geologists Bull., v. 54, p. 469-486.

Gellatly, D.C., 1970, Cross-bedded tidal megaripples from King Sound (Northwestern Australia); Sedimentary Geology, v. 4, p. 185-191.

Goldring, R., 1971, Shallow-water sedimentation as illustrated in the Upper Devonian Baggy Beds: Geol. Soc. London Mem. 5, 80 p.

Houbolt, J.J.C., 1968, Recent sediments in the southern Bight of the North Sea: Geol. en Mijnb, v. 47, p. 245-273.

Klein, G.deV., 1963, Bay of Fundy intertidal zone sediments: Jour. Sedimentary Petrology, v. 33, p. 844-854.

_____, 1967, Paleocurrent analysis in relation to modern marine sediment dispersal patterns: Am. Assoc. Petroleum Geologists Bull., v. 51, p. 366-381.

_____, 1970a, Depositional and dispersal dynamics of intertidal sand bars: Jour. Sedimentary Petrology, v. 40, p. 1095-1127.

_____, 1970b, Tidal origin of a Precambrian quartzite--The Lower Fine-grained Quartzite (Dalradian) of Islay, Scotland: Jour. Sedimentary Petrology, v. 40, p. 973-985.

_____, 1970c, Paleotidal sedimentation (Abs.): Geol. Soc. Abs. with Programs, v. 2, p. 598.

_____, 1971, A sedimentary model for determining paleotidal range: Geol. Soc. America Bull., v. 82, p. 2585-2592.

_____, 1972a, Sedimentary model for determining paleotidal range: reply: Geol. Soc. America Bull., v. 83, p. 539-546.

_____, 1972b, Determination of paleotidal range in clastic sedimentary rocks: XXIV Int. Geol. Congress Rept. Sect. 6, p. 397-405.

_____, 1976, Holocene tidal sedimentation: Stroudsburg, PA, Dowden, Hutchinson & Ross, Inc.

Klein, G.deV, and Whaley, Margaret L., 1972, Hydraulic parameters controlling bedform migration on an intertidal sand body: Geol. Soc. America Bull, v. 83, p. 3465-3470.

McCave, I.N., 1970, Deposition of fine-grained suspended sediment from tidal currents: Jour. Geophysical Research, v. 75, p. 4151-4159.

Michaelis, E.R. and Dixon, G., 1969, Interpretation of depositional processes from sedimentary structures in the Cardium Sand: Canadian Petroleum Geology Bull., v. 17, p. 410-443.

Narayan, J., 1971, Sedimentary structures in the Lower Greensand of the Weald, England and Bas-Boulonnais, France: Sedimentary Geology, v. 6, p. 73-109.

Phillips, W.E.A., 1974, The stratigraphy, sedimentary environments and paleogeography of the Silurian strata of Clare Island, Co. Mayo, Ireland: Jour. Geol. Soc. London, v. 130, p. 19-41.

Pryor, W.A., 1970, Petrology of the Weissliegende Sandstones in the Harz and Werra-Fulda areas, Germany: Geol. Rundschau., v. 60, p. 524-552.

Pryor, W.A., 1971, Petrology of the Permian Yellow Sands of northeastern England and their North Sea Basin equivalents: Sedimentary Geology, v. 6, p. 221-254.

Redfield, A.C., 1958, The influence of the continental shelf on the tides of the Atlantic Coast of the United States: Jour. Marine Res., v. 17, p. 432-448.

Reineck, H.E., 1963, Sedimentgefuge in Bereich der sudliche Nordsee: Senckengergische Naturf. Gesell. Abh., No. 505, p. 1-138.

_____, 1967, Layered sediments of tidal flats, beaches and shelf bottoms, p. 191-206: in Lauff, G.H., editor, Estuaries: Am. Assoc. Adv. Sci. Pub. 83.

Shinn, E.A., 1973, Sedimentary accretion along the leeward, SE coast
of Qatar Peninsula, Persian Gulf, p. 199-209: in Purser, N.H.,
editor, 1973, The Persian Gulf: New York, Springer-Verlag, 471 p.

Stride, A.H., 1963, Current-swept sea floors near the southern half
of Great Britian: Geol. Soc. London Quar, Jour., v. 119,
p. 175-199.

Swett, Keene, Klein, G.deV., and Smit, D.E., 1971, A Cambrian tidal sand
body--The Eriboll Sandstone of northwest Scotland: an ancient-Recent
analog: Jour. Geology, v. 79, p. 400-415.

Thompson, R.W., 1968, Tidal flat sedimentation on the Colorado River
Delta, northwestern Gulf of California: Geol. Soc. America
Mem. 107, 133 p.

Van Straaten, L.M.J.U., 1952, Biogene textures and the formation of
shell beds in the Dutch Wadden Sea: Koninkl. Nederlandse Akad.
Wtensch. Proc. Ser.B, v. 55, p. 500-516.

_____, 1954, Sedimentology of Recent Tidal flat deposits and the
Psammites du Condroz (Devonian): Geol. en. Mijnb, v. 16, p. 25-47.

Verger, Fernand, 1968, Marais et wadden du littoral Francais: Bordeaux,
Biscaye Frerees Imprimeurs, 541 p.

Weber, K.J., 1971, Sedimentological aspects of oil fields in the Niger
Delta: Geol. en. Minjnb., v. 50, p. 559-576.

Wunderlich, F., 1970, Genesis and evnironment of the "Nellenkopfen-
schichten" "Lower Emsian, Rheinian Devonian) at locus typicus
in comparison with modern coastal environments of the German
Bay: Jour. Sedimentary Petrology, v. 40, p. 102-130.

4 DELTAS

INTRODUCTION

Of the various depositional models to be discussed in this course, deltas represent the most complex and composite type of sand bodies. The complexity is a result of the differential interplay of fluvial input, wave and tidal action, sediment dispersal, tectonic setting, and a variety of other factors which influence the style of deltaic sedimentation.

Deltas occur where river systems empty into a standing body of water, a lake or an ocean. Their occurrence at such a location is due to the sudden decrease in hydraulic gradient.

The morphology of a delta is fan-shaped in plan and lenticular in cross-section. Geometrically, deltas differ from an alluvial and a submarine fan which are wedge-shaped in cross-section.

A genetic classification of deltas is proposed according to the relative intensity of fluvial discharge, wave action and tidal current systems, and an example of each is shown (Table 2). Galloway (1975) has classified the world's deltas according to such a scheme also (Figure 64).

DEPOSITIONAL HYDRAULICS OF RIVER-DOMINATED DELTAS

The following four depositional processes operate in deltaic environments: river input, tidal action, wind-driven waves and resulting longshore currents, and density (or turbidity) currents. The Bates theory of jet flow for delta formation was proposed in 1953 and has guided North American thinking concerning river-dominated deltas. The Bates model assumes that river flow into the ocean is comparable to discharge of a turbulent fluid through a well-defined stable orifice (Figure 65). This jet flow is either two-dimensional or three demensional, referred to as plane jet and axial jet, respectively. Three types of jet flows are recognized according to differences in density contrast between the jet flow itself and the ambient fluid into which it flows.

TABLE 2. Variability of deltaic type according to relative
interplay of fluvial input, wave action and tidal
action.

Processes	Mississippi Delta	Senegal Delta	Niger Delta	Klang- Langat Delta	Ord River Delta
River Input	High	Low	Moderate	Low to Moderate	Low
Wave Intensity	Moderate	Extreme	Moderate	Low	Low
Tidal Action	Low	Low	Moderate	Strong	Extreme
Delta Type	River- Dominated Delta	Wave- Domin- ated Delta	Balanced Delta	Tide- Domin- ated Delta	Tide- Domin- ated Delta

SOURCES OF DATA FOR TABLE 2. Mississippi Delta (Fisk, 1961; Gould,
1970), Senegal Delta (Coleman and Wright, 1975), Niger Delta
(Allen, 1970; Omkens, 1974), Klang-Langat Delta, Malaysia, (Coleman
et al, 1970), Ord River Delta, Australia, (Coleman et al, 1972).

Hyperpycnal Inflow

This type of flow is a plane jet oriented vertically. The inflowing river water is more dense than the surrounding oceanic or lake water. It moves along the ocean floor, acquires rapid acceleration, erodes material on the delta front, cuts delta front troughs (or submarine canyons) and deposits sediment at the foot of the delta where gradients decline. Expressed in another way, this kind of jet flow is a turbidity current.

Homopycnal Inflow

This flow is an axial jet, where the denisty of the inflowing river is almost equal to that of the ambient water of an ocean or lake. It is more common in lakes than along an ocean. It produces a classical Gilbert-type delta.

Hypopycnal Inflow

This flow is a plane jet oriented in a horizontal plane. The inflowing river water is less dense that the surrounding ocean water into which it flows. The ocean water is more dense because of its salinity and its colder temperature. Tidal currents amplify the density contrast at the river mouth by incursion of a wedge of saline water into the river mouth. The sea water then buoys up the river water and its suspended sediment content. Tidal action and wave action flushes this supended clay into interdistributary bays, although some of this clay is also deposited by suspension settlement onto the ocean floor. The type of delta generated by this process is an imbricating delta.

More recently, Wright and Coleman (1974) have observed the changes in flow conditions of such hypopycnal jet flow at the mouth of the Mississippi Delta. There, the size and areal dimension of the effluent jet flow changes with each phase of the tidal cycle (Figure 66). In addition, the density of the water shifts concurrently, and during the ebb phase of the tidal cycle, concentrates over the distributary mouth bar (Figure 67). Once the effluent jet flow moves seaward over the bar, it expands and loses velocity and hydraulic effectiveness. As a consequence maximum reworking of sediment occurs on the crest of the distributary mouth bar and thus accounts for its excellent reservoir properties. This reworking is also enhanced by the intersection of the bar crest with the near-horizontal boundary between the effluent jet flow and the ambient ocean water along which internal waves move landward and break along the bar crest.

MISSISSIPPI DELTA (RIVER-DOMINATED)

The Mississippi Delta is the type example of a river-dominated delta. Most of the discussion that follows is taken from Fisk et al (1954), Fisk (1956), and Fisk (1961), Gould (1970), Morgan et al (1968), Coleman and Gagliano (1965), Huang and Goodell (1970) Scruton (1956, 1960), and Wright and Coleman (1974).

The plan of the Mississippi Delta is that of a birdfoot (Figure 29). The most landward zone is an alluvial plain characterized by meandering channels, levees and a floodplain that has dominant swamp vegetation. This zone grades into the upper deltaic plain which is generally non-marine and is separated from the lower deltaic plain by the position of maximum inland inflow of salt water by tidal processes. Here channels consist of sand, grading laterally into silty levees, and an interchannel zone of mud and marsh. The lower deltaic plain is traversed by a distributary channel network. Here, the channels diverge from the main channel and lace their way through the muds of the interdistirbutary bays (Figures 69, 70, 71). The geometry of the channel sands is shoestring and bifurcating in the downslope direction (Figure 71). The channels are bounded by levees which separate the channels from the interdistributary bays. The bays are areas of mud deposition and marsh growth; the mud is supplied by crevasse splays and overbank flowing during flooding, or redispersal of mud from the ocean back into the bay by wave and tidal action.

At the mouth of the distributary channels thick and coarse deposits of sand are formed. These are known as distributary mouth bars formed due to dumping action of sand where river outflow enters the ocean. Wave action reworks these sands and longshore current systems redistribute this sand as linear sand bars oriented parallel to the depositional strike (Figure 72 and 73). Internal waves, occurring as an interface between effluent from the river (hypopycnal inflow) and more dense Gulf waters, rework the surface of the bars, enhancing its sorting and porosity during the ebb phase of a tidal cycle (Figure 67). These bars prograde seaward with distributary progradation (Figure 73). Bar morphology and sediments are zoned with respect to depositional processes (Figure 74).

Seaward of the mouth bars is the delta front environment. This zone consists of interbedded sands and mud.

Seaward is the prodelta zone an area of predominant mud deposition.

The growth and development of the Mississippi Delta appears to go through alternations of constructional and destructional events (Scruton, 1960). During the constructional phase, delta outbuilding procedes by the seaward progradation of distributary channels (average rate of 80 m per year). The inter-distributary bays prograde in association with channel progradation, as does the prodelta zone by mud suspension deposition. However, the efficiency of these extended channels is limited, and as they extend too far, the main channels of the Mississippi jump and divert through a shorter course to the ocean. This process has created the imbricate deltaic plain of South Louisiana. The imbricate model gives a composite delta consisting of a series of lenticular packets.

Following channel shifting, the abandoned delta goes through a destructive phase as the sediment supply is cut off. The older distributaries slowly fill in with fine sediments (e.g. Plaquemines - St. Bernard Delta; Bayou Larose) and subsidence causes the older delta plain to sink below sea level. At this stage, wave action redistributes sand from the delta edge and the older distributary channels into a system of barrier islands (Chandelier Islands). These sands are preserved under transgressive marine shales.

Seaward progradation of distributary channels and sedimentary imbalance caused by rapid dumping of distributary mouth bar sands over water-saturated prodelta muds, forces shale diapiric structures to upwell in front of the mouth bars. These diapiric structures are known as mud lumps.

NIGER DELTA (BALANCED)

The data dealing with this delta come from work by Allen (1965, 1970) and a more recent paper by Oomkens (1974). The Niger Delta has a high sand content with a high discharge of 2 x 10^{11} m^3/annum. Sand transport rate is 2 x 10^{11}m^3 per annum. Wave action generated from a fetch across the south Atlantic is moderate to high. The tidal range averages 2.2 meters, which is moderate, but still significant. The external morphology is symmetrical, and in plan looks like a hammer head. Here, the delta plain consists of braided distributaries filled with sand, lacing through muds and mangrove swamps. The seaward edge of the delta plain consists of barrier islands cut by tidal channels (Figure 75). The prodelta zone and delta front zone is similar to the Mississippi (Figure 75).

KLANG-LANGAT DELTA (TIDE-DOMINATED)

This delta has been described by Coleman et al (1970). Here, two small rivers, the Klang and the Langat merge to form a delta. The discharge of these rivers is relatively low, as is the wave action. Tidal range, however, is up to 4.28 meters (Figure 76). The delta plain consists of tidal shoals, tidal channels and tidal flats (Figure 77). Here, the tidal channels fill the role of transporting sand in much the same way as distributary channels transport sand in the Mississippi. Levees are absent. Seaward of the delta edge of tidal shoals are delta front and prodelta sediments similar to those of the Mississippi and the Niger.

OTHER DELTAS

A detailed discussion of other deltas from which a modern sedimentological base has been developed is to be found in Coleman and Wright (1975). Both the areal distribution and vertical sequence of sediments in the Senegal, Sao Francisco, Ord and Burdekin Deltas are included there.

DELTAIC VERTICAL SEQUENCE

For most deltas, the vertical sequence of sedimentary structures, lithologies and textures is coarsening-upward (Figure 78). Despite the style of sedimentation, all deltas show such a sequence except for the delta plain portion which will be variable. Thus the top of the sequence of a prograding river-dominated delta will consist of distributary channels and levees and interdistributary bays (Figure 78), whereas the Niger-type of delta consists of a top with channels, barrier islands and tidal channels (Figure 78). A tide-dominated delta consists of a coarsening-upward sequence capped by tidal shoals, tidal channels and tidal flats. The tidal-flat portion would locally fine-upward (Figure 78). A wave-dominated delta like the Senegal delta would be capped with a barrier island sand sheet, and perhaps be difficult to tell from the coarsening-upward sequence generated by a prograding coastline like the Texas Coast (See Coleman and Wright, 1975).

GRAVITY PROCESSES ON DELTAS

Most deltaic environments are characterized by slope instability which generates slumping. In addition, diapirism is not uncommon (Morgan et al, 1968) and occurs in many deltas, such as the Magdelena delta of Columbia (Shepard, 1973). There, diapirism triggers off large slumps and slides (Figures 79 and 80). These slides leave behind delta front troughs which funnel turbidity currents and sand flows. An ancient example similar to the Magdelena was described by Klein et al (1972) from the Cretaceous Reconcavo Basin of Brazil. There, the slumping and subaqueous gravity processes obliterated primary porosity in sand bodies and drove off any petroleum stored in such sands, or prevented oil migration. Such slumped masses may, however, make an effective permeability seal.

ANCIENT DELTAS

The Pennsylvanian rocks of the Appalachian Plateau of the eastern USA contain some classic examples of ancient deltaic sequences (Ferm, 1962, 1975; Ferm and Williams, 1963, 1964) with extremely complex river channel patterns associated within these deltas. Another classic example is the Devonian of New York, whose deltaic origin was reognized near the turn of this century by Barrel. The Caseyville Formation, as well as other Pennsylvanian units in the Illinois Basin, is another example of a deltaic facies (Wanless et al, 1970). The Cretaceous appears to be another period of extensive deltaic development particularly in the Rocky Mountains of the USA where, amongst many units, the Parkman Sandstone of Wyoming (Hubert et al, 1972) and the Frontier Formation of Wyoming have all the classical coarsening-upward successions predicted from the Mississippi (Figure 81). Deltas have also been described from the Atoka Formation (Pennsylvanian) of Oklahoma, the Abbotsham Formation (DeRaaf et al, 1965) and the Wilcox Group (Eocene) of Texas. These examples represent just a partial list of deltaic sedimentary rocks (See also Morgan, 1970, Broussard, 1975, and Shirley, 1966 for other examples).

OIL FIELD EXAMPLES

Deltas are one of the four major environments of deposition from which oil is produced and exploited. There are many examples of which the Booch Sandstone (Pennsylvanian) of Oklahoma is perhaps the most widely cited one (Figure 82). The Wilcox Group of Texas is another prolific oil producer (Figure 83, 84, 85 86). One of the best examples of hydro-carbon production from ancient deltaic sediments is the total post-Cretaceous sedimentary section of the Gulf Coast where deltaic sands form the reservoir rocks. These are trapped in a variety of salt domes and growth fault

type traps.   Prodelta,   bay   and lagoonal shales provide the
source and seal   rocks.   Cenozoic   sequences of. Niger Delta
produce from deltaic sequences exactly similar to that of the
Gulf Coast (Weber 1971).   Production has   also been obtained
from deltaic   sand bodies in the Parkman (Cretaceous) and
Frontier (Cretaceous) formations of Wyoming.

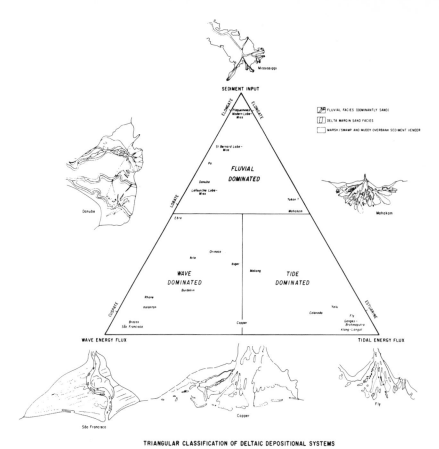

FIGURE 64. Ternary classification of deltas according to dominant depositional mode (From Galloway, 1975; Reprinted by permission of the Houston Geological Society).

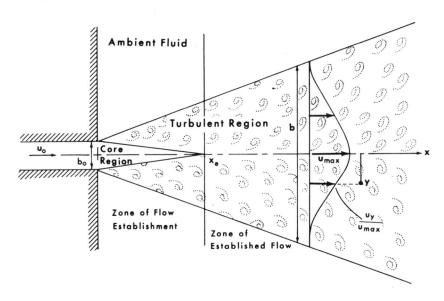

FIGURE 65. Definition of zones for turbulent jet flow model (From Wright and Coleman, 1964; Reprinted by permission of the University of Chicago Press).

76

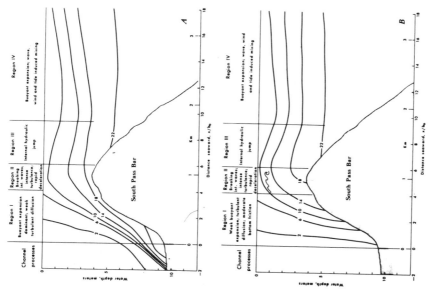

FIGURE 67. Density cross-sections of flow systems at South Pass, Mississippi Delta during rising river stage, January 31, 1973. A-flood tide. B- ebb tide. (from Wright and Coleman, 1974; Reprinted by permission of the University of Chicago Press).

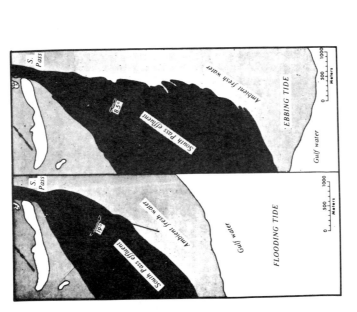

FIGURE 66. Relationships between South pass effluent and ambient water masses during flooding and ebbing tide, Mississippi Delta (From Wright and Coleman, 1974; Reprinted by permission of the University of Chicago Press).

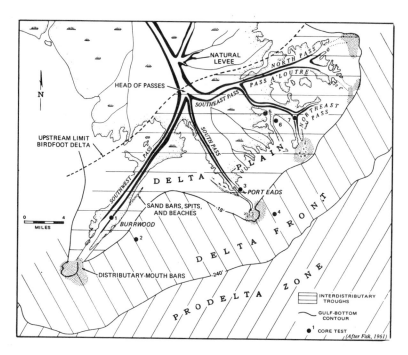

FIGURE 68. Depositional environments and subenvironments, Mississippi Birdfoot Delta (From Gould, 1970, after Fisk, 1961; Reprinted by permission of the Society of Economic Paleontologist and Mineralogists).

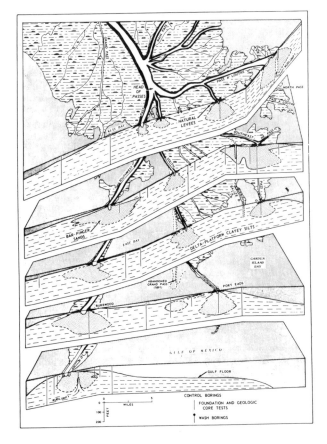

FIGURE 69. Model of Mississippi Birdfoot delta showing geometry of distributary channel systems (From Fisk, 1961; Reprinted by permission of the American Association of Petroleum Geologists).

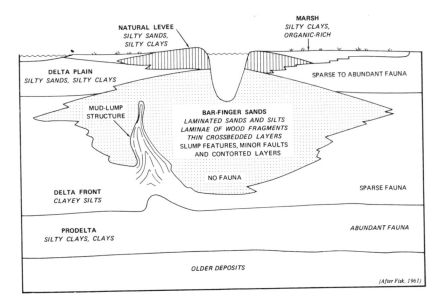

FIGURE 70. Cross-section of a typical bar-finger sand showing characteristic features and associated facies (From Gould, 1970; after Fisk, 1961). Mississippi delta (Reprinted by permission of the Society of Economic Paleontologists and Mineralogists).

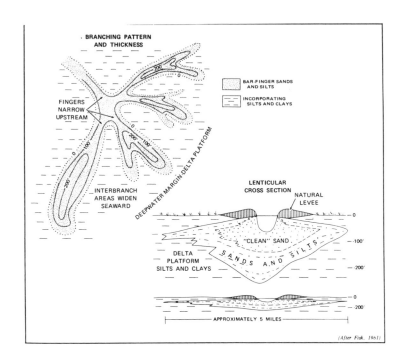

FIGURE 71. Geometry and sedimentary characteristics of Mississippi Delta bar finger sands (From Gould, 1970; after Fisk, 1961; Reprinted by permission of the Society of Economic Paleontologists and Mineralogists).

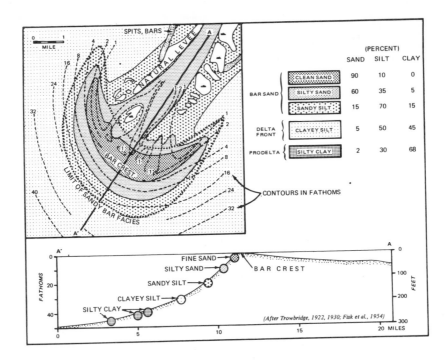

FIGURE 72. Relationship of sediment facies distribution in distributary channels and distributary mouth bars of Mississippi Delta (From Gould, 1970; Reprinted by permission of the Society of Economic Paleontologists and Mineralogists).

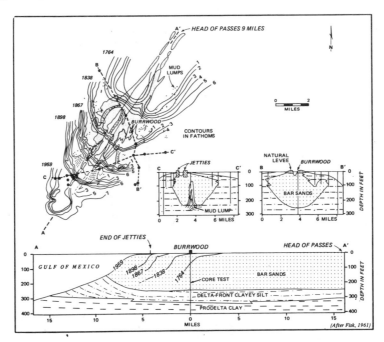

FIGURE 73. Historic development of progradation of Southwest Pass bar finger, Mississippi Delta (from Gould, 1970; reprinted by permission of the Society of Economic Paleontologists and Mineralogists).

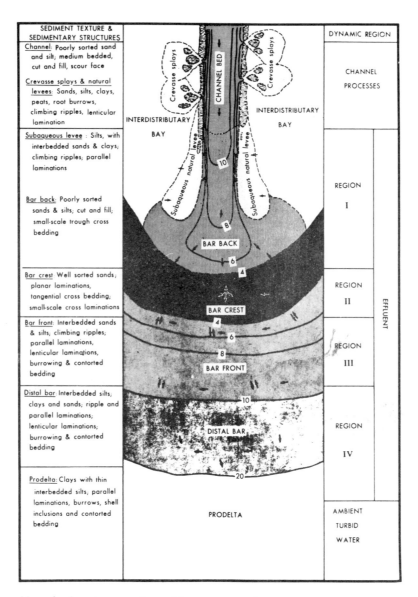

FIGURE 74. Morphologic and sedimentary characteristics of a stratified river mouth and relationships to effluent dynamic regions (from Wright and Coleman, 1974; reprinted by permission of the University of Chicago Press).

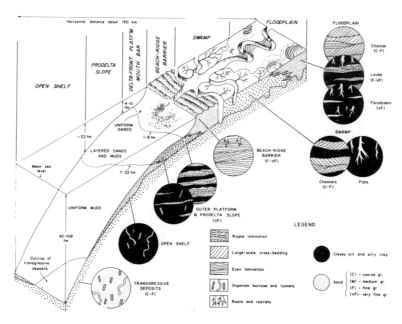

FIGURE 75. Principle sedimentary facies of the Holocene Niger Delta (from Allen, 1970; reprinted by permission of the Society of Economic Paleontologists and Mineralogists).

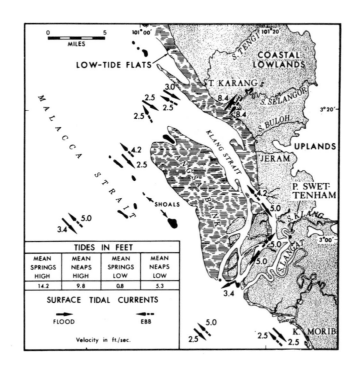

FIGURE 76. Klang-Langat Delta--major physiographic zones, environments, tidal ranges and tidal currents (from Coleman, et al., 1970; reprinted by permission of the Society of Economic Paleontologists and Mineralogists).

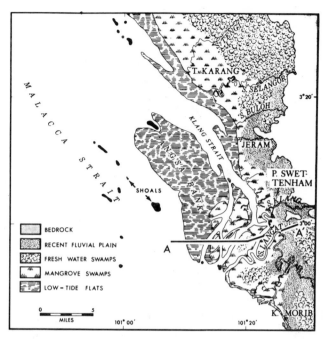

FIGURE 77. Klang-Langat Delta, Malaysia, showing depositional environments (from Coleman, et al., 1970; reprinted by permission of the Society of Economic Paleontologists and Mineralogists).

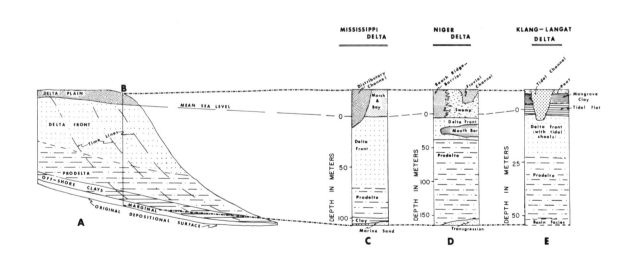

FIGURE 78. Vertical and lateral distribution of sediments on idealized delta based on vertical succession of deltaic subenvironments (A). (B) position of vertical squence on ideal delta in columns C, D, E. (C) Mississippi Delta. (D) Niger Delta. (E) Klang-Langat Delta (from Klein, 1974; reprinted by permission of the Geological Society of America).

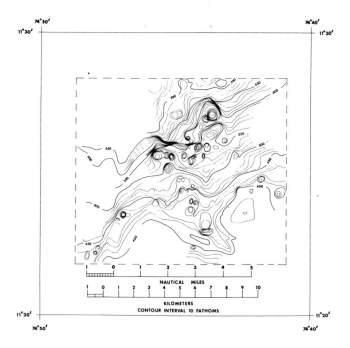

FIGURE 79. Magdelena Delta, Columbia, showing principle area of diapirism (from Shepard, 1973; reprinted by permission of the Geological Society of America).

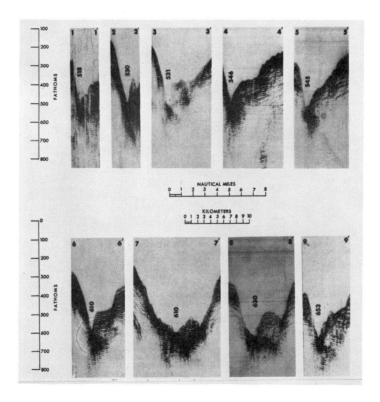

FIGURE 80. Magdelena Delta, Columbia, Seismic profiles showing slump topography terracing on slump blocks and slump faults (from Shepard, 1973; reprinted by permission of the Geological Society of America).

<u>FIGURE 81</u>. Coarsening-upward sequence produced by prograding delta, Frontier Formation (Cretaceous), North Tisdale, Wyoming. 1) Delta Plain distributary sandstone; 2) Delta Front; 3) Prodelta (reprinted by permission of the Geological Society of America).

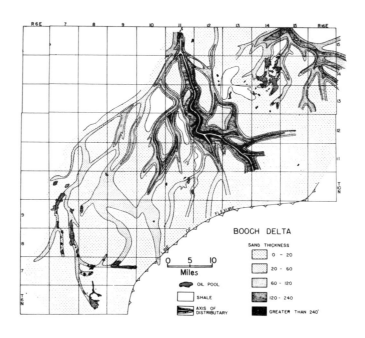

<u>FIGURE 82</u>. Sandstone isopachs defining distributary channel system in Pennsylvanian Booch Sandstones, of deltaic origin, Oklahoma (from Busch, 1959; reprinted by permission of the American Association of Petroleum Geologists).

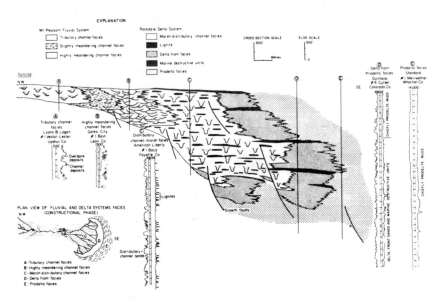

FIGURE 83. Rockdale Delta System Wilcox Group, Texas (from Fisher and McGowen, 1969; reprinted by permission of the American Association of Petroleum Geologists).

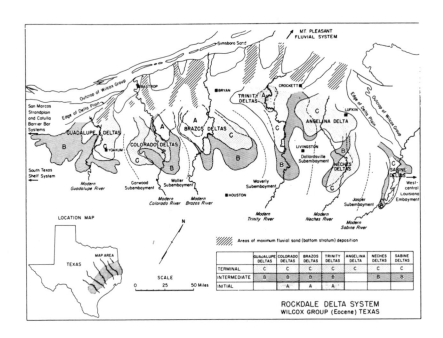

FIGURE 84. Distribution of principle deltas in Wilcox Group, Texas (from Fisher and McGowen, 1969; reprinted by permission of the American Association of Petroleum Geologists).

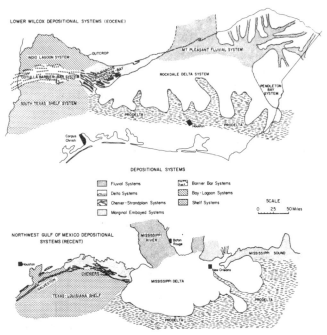

FIGURE 85. Comparison of Lower Wilcox deltaic depositional system (Eocene) and northern Gulf of Mexico (Holocene), (from Fisher and McGowen, 1969; reprinted by permission of the American Association of Petroleum Geologists).

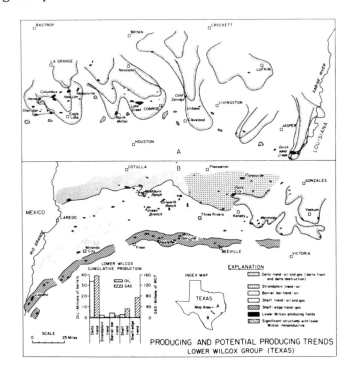

FIGURE 86. Productive and potentially productive oil and gas trends, Lower Wilcox Group (Eocene), Texas (from Fisher and McGowen, 1969; reprinted by permission of the American Association of Petroleum Geologists).

SELECTED BIBLIOGRAPHY

Allen, J.R.L., 1965, Late Quaternary Niger Delta and adjacent areas: Am. Assoc. Petroleum Geologists Bull., v. 49, p. 547-600.

_____, 1970, Sediments of the modern Niger Delta, p. 138-151: in Morgan, J.P., ed, 1970, Deltaic sedimentation: modern and ancient: Soc. Econ. Paleontologists and Mineralogists Spec. Pub. 15, 312 p.

Bates, C.C., 1953, Rational theory of delta formation: Am. Assoc. Petroleum Geologists, Bull., v. 37, p. 2119-2162.

Broussard, M.L., editor, 1975, Deltas, 2nd ed: Houston, TEX, Houston Geol. Soc., 555 p.

Busch, D.A., 1959, Prospecting for stratigraphic traps: Am. Assoc. Petroleum Geologists Bull., v. 43, p. 2829-2843.

Coleman, J.M. and Gagliano, S.M., 1965, Sedimentary structures-Mississippi Delta Plain, p. 133-148: in Middleton, G.V., editor, 1965, Primary sedimentary structures and their hydrodynamic interpretation--a symposium: Soc. Econ. Paleontologists and Mineralogists Spec. Pub. 12, 265 p.

Coleman, J.M., Gagliano, S.M. and Smith, W.G., 1970, Sedimentation in a Malaysian high tide tropical delta, p. 185-197: in Morgan, J.P., editor, 1970, Deltaic sedimentation: modern and ancient: Soc. Econ. Paleontologists and Mineralogists Spec. Pub. 15, 312 p.

Coleman, J.M., and Wright, L.D., 1975, Modern river deltas: variability of processes and sand bodies, p. 99-150: in Broussard, M.L., editor, 1975, Deltas, 2nd ed: Houston, Houston. Geol. Soc., 555p.

DeRaaf, J.F.M., Reading, H.G., and Walker, R.G., 1965, Cyclic sedimentation in the Lower Westphalian of North Devon, England: Sedimentology, v. 4, p. 1-52.

Edelman, C.H., 1965, Sedimentology of the Rhine and Meuse Deltas as an example of the sedimentology of the Carboniferous: Geol. en. Mijnb, v. 16, p. 64-75.

Ferm, J.C., 1962, Petrology of some Pennsylvanian sedimentary rocks: Jour. Sedimentary Petrology, v. 32, p. 104123.

_____, 1970, Allegheny deltaic deposits, p. 246255: in Morgan, J.P., editor, 1970, Deltaic sedimentation: modern and ancient: Soc. Econ. Paleontologists and Mineralogists Spec. Pub 15, 312 p.

_____, 1974, Carboniferous environmental models in eastern
   United States and their significance, p. 79-95: in Briggs,
   Garrett, Editor, 1974, CArboniferous of the southeastern United
   States: Geol. Soc. America Spec. Pub 148, 361 p.

Ferm, J.C., and Williams, E.G., 1963, Model for Cyclic sedimentation
   in the Appalachian Pennsylvanian, Amer. Assoc. of Pet. Geol.
   Bull., Vol. 47, No. 2 p. 356.

Ferm, J.C., and Williams, E.G., 1964, Sedimentary facies in the
   lower Allegheny rocks of western Pennsylvania, Jour. Sed. Pet.,
   Vol. 34, p. 610-614.

Fisher, W.L., and McGowen, J.H., 1969, Depositional systems in
   Wilcox Group (Eocene) of Texas and their relation to occurence
   of oil and gas: Am Assoc Petroleum Geologists Bull., v. 53, p. 30-54.

Fisk, H.N., 1956, Nearshore sediments of the Continental Shelf off
   Louisiana: Proc. Eighth Texas Conf. on Soil Mechanics and
   Foundation Engineering, p. 1-23.

_____, 1961, Bar-finger sands of the Mississippi Delta, p. 29-52:
   in Peterson, J.A. and Osmund, J.C., editors, 1961, Geometry of
   sandstone bodies: Am. Assoc. Petroleum Geologists, 240 p.

Fisk, H.N., McFarlan, E., Jr., Kolb, C.R. and Wilbert, L.J., Jr.,
   1954, Sedimentary framework of the modern Mississippi Delta:
   Jour. Sedimentary Petrology, v. 24, p. 76-99.

Galloway, W.E., 1975, Process framework for describing the morphological and stratigraphic evolution of deltaic depositional
   systems, p. 87-98: in Broussard, M.L., editor, 1975, Deltas,
   2nd ed: Houston, Houston Geol. Soc., 555 p.

Gould, H.R. 1970, The Mississippi Delta Complex, p. 3-30: in Morgan,
   J.P., editor, 1970, Deltaic sedimentation: modern and ancient:
   Soc. Econ. Paleontologists and Mineralogists Spec. Pub. 15,
   312 p.

Huang, T.C., and Goodell, H.G., 1970, Sediments and sedimentary processes of eastern Mississippi Cone, Gulf of Mexico:; Am. Assoc.
   Petroleum Geologists Bull., v. 54, p. 2070-2100.

Hubert, J.F., Butera, J.G., and Rice, R.F., 1972, Sedimentology
   of the Upper Cretaceous Cody-Parkman Delta, southwestern Powder
   River Basin, Wyoming: Geol. Soc. America Bull., v. 83, p. 1649-1670.

Klein, G.deV, 1974, Estimating water depths from analysis of
   barrier island and deltaic sedimentary sequences: Geology, v. 2,
   p. 409-412.

Klein, G.deV, DeMelo, U., and Della Favera, J.C., 1972, Subaqueous
    gravity processes on the front of Cretaceous deltas, Reconcavo
    Basin, Brazil: Geol. Soc. America Bull, v. 83, p. 1469-1492.

Morgan, J.P., editor, 1970, Deltaic sedimentation: modern and
    ancient: Soc. Econ. Paleontologists and Mineralogists Spec.
    Pub. 15, 312 p.

Morgan, J.P., Coleman, J.M., and Gagliano, S.M., 1968, Mudlumps:
    diapiric structures in Mississippi Delta sediments, p. 145-161:
    in Braunstein, Jules, editor, 1968, Diapirs and diapirism: Am.
    Assoc. Petroleum Geologists Mem. 8.

Oomkens, E., 1974, Lithofacies relations in the Late Quaternary
    Niger Delta complex: Sedimentology, v. 21, p. 195-221.

Scruton, P.C., 1956, Oceanography of Mississippi Delta sedimentary
    environments: Am. Assoc. Petroleum Geologists Bull., v. 40, p. 2864-2952.

_____, 1960, Delta building and the deltaic sequence, p. 82-102:
    in Shepard, F.P., Rhleger, F.B. and Van Andel, Tj.H, editors,
    1960, Recent sediments, northwest Gulf of Mexico: Am. Assoc.
    Petroleum Geologists, 394 p.

Shepard, F.P., 1973, Sea floor of Magdelena Delta and Santa Marta
    area, Columbia: Geol. Soc. America Bull., v. 84, p. 1955-1972.

Shirley, M.L., editor, 1966, Deltas: Houston, Texas; Houston Geol.
    Soc., 251 p.

Taylor, J.H., 1962, Sedimentary features of an ancient deltaic com-
    plex: The Wealden Rocks of southeastern England: Sedimentology,
    Vol. 2, pp. 2-28.

Visher, G. S., 1965, Fluvial processes interpreted from ancient and
    recent fluvial deposits: in Primary sedimentary structures and
    thier hydrodynamic interpretation (Middleton, G. V., editor)
    Soc. of Econ. Paleongologists and Mineralogists, Spec. Pub.
    No. 12, pp. 133-148.

Wanless, H.R., et al, 1970, Late Paleozoic deltas in the central
    and eastern United States, p. 215-245: in Morgan, J.P., editor,
    1970, Deltaic sedimentation: modern and ancient: Soc. Econ.
    Paleontologists and Mineralogists Spec. Pub. 15, 312 p.

Weber, K.J., 1971, Sedimentological aspects of oil fields in the
    Niger Delta: Geol. en Mijnb, v. 50, p. 559-576.

Wright, L.D., and Coleman, J.M., 1974, Mississippi River mouth pro-
    cesses: effluent dynamics and morphologic development: Jour.
    Geology, v. 82, p. 751-778.

5

TURBIDITES

INTRODUCTION

Turbidite sedimentation owes its origin to subaqueous gravity flow processes in deep water marine environments. These processes are diverse (Figure 87) but they all constitute part of a continuum. Middleton and Hampton (1973) have classified subaqueous depositional systems into four classes (Figure 87) and their nomenclature is adopted herein. Although the four processes they recognize are part of a continuum they differ according to support mechanisms for sediment transport and types of sedimentary deposits. Turbidites are part of that continuum.

Although this discussion will focus on the subaqueous gravity sedimentation processes in deep water marine environments, it must be emphasized that their occurrence is not confined exclusively to the ocean basin floors, continental margins or submarine fans. Turbidity currents and submarine slumps are common in deltaic settings. Turbidity currents (hyperpycnal jet inflow) occur off the Mississippi Delta during spring flooding (Scruton, 1956) and large scale slumps have been recorded off the Magdelena delta (Shepard, 1973). An ancient analog of such sedimentation has been documented from a Cretaceous deltaic system in the Reconcavo Basin, Brazil by Klein et al (1972). Thus, our discussion has relevance to deltaic settings also. A brief discussion of the four different type of flows that transport sands into the deeper water marine environments is given below.

GRAVITY PROCESSES

Debris Flow (Hampton, 1972

Debris flows are sediment-water mixutres which move along shear planes within the body of the material. These shear planes provide ways for material to move downslope. Some of this mass moves as a rigid plug bounded by a zone along which shearing and movement occurs. Deformation of the material is internal. Debris flow refers, therefore, to sluggish movements downslope of mixed granular solids, clay minerals and water in response to gravity.

The granular solids (mostly sand and gravel) in a debris flow are transported and supported by the interstitial mixtures of clay and water. This process provides a support mechanism of "matrix strength" (clay minerals and water combined in fluid style) with a limited cohesive strength. This strength supports the floating grains of sand and gravel. The clay-water fluid has excess density with respect to normal water, giving the debris flow greater buoyancy to support sand and gravel. Competence of the debris flow is a function, then, of the strength and density of the clay-water mixture. Consequently, the greater the density, the coarser the granular solids that are transported. Once density diminishes, so does the largest grain size that the debris flows can transport.

The solids of sand and gravel are transported by a process of dispersion. This means that each of the grains exert a dispersive stress provided by continual grain collision. The resulting sediments are of mixed grain sizes ranging from very fine-grained to extremely coarse. A fabric of coarser grains floating in finer grains is the result. Stratification is non-existent.

Deposition occurs by a process of mass emplacement. Thus, textures appear like that of tillites and pebbly mudstones. Klein et al (1972) illustrated the type of deposition that can occur under this process in their category of "mass flow" facies. These deposits are massive and structureless, although slide marks may occur on the soles of beds. Pull-aparts may occur as sediment becomes progressively fluidized by the ambient water and loses cohesion.

Vertical sequences produced from this type of flow are not clearly understood. A suggested sequence proposed by Middleton and Hampton (1973) is shown in Figure 88.

Grain Flow (Middleton and Hampton, 1973)

The concept of grain flow was proposed by R. A. Bagnold (1954) to indicate a mechanism whereby upward supporting stress acts on grains within flowing sediments because of grain-to-grain collisions. This stress is grain-dispersive stress and is proportional to the shear stress transmitted between grains. It prevents grains from being deposited out of flows. An example of the kind of flow Bagnold had in mind is sand avalanching down the slip face of an eolian dune where the pull of gravity moves the grains along. Support is provided by grain interaction.

These kinds of flows have been reported by Shepard and Dill from the upper ends of submarine canyons; Dill has demonstrated this process with movie observations. These flows were termed by them as "Rivers of Sand"; these sand flows are strong enough to erode submarine canyons and the dispersive stresses are strong enough to support gravel.

The depositional mechanism is, again, mass emplacement. The boundary of sedimentary deposits so emplaced, is sharp and deposits are thick. The fabric consists of dispersed clasts of pebbles floating in sand, and the sediment texture ranges from clay to gravel (Klein, et al, 1972). The base of the beds may include sole marks, slide marks and load structures, and internally, may include dish structures. Stauffer (1967) interpreted the dish structure to be produced by grain flow, although more recent work by Lowe and LePiccolo (1974) indicates that they were formed by water-escape. Such water escape occurs after grain flow ceases.

Reverse graded bedding may also occur in such sediments.

The type of vertical sequence generated by grain flows is shown in Figure 88 (Middleton and Hampton, 1973).

Fluidized Sediment Flow (Middleton and Hampton, 1973)

This type of gravity flow involves the expansion of a bed of sediment by the introduction of fluids within the pore spaces and the fluid flow is such that both it, the fluid, and the grains are moved upward. In other words, the sediment becomes liquified like quick sand. It requires loose grain packing of sand to overcome the resistence of grain fabric to fluid injection. The supporting mechanism for this process is excess pore pressure of interstitial fluid that keeps the sedimentary particles afloat. Gravity propels the fluidized sediment down slope. A high concentration of sediment with excess pore pressure is mandatory to induce this flow mechanism.

To keep the fluidized sediment in transport, pore pressures must exceed hydrostatic pressures and the sediment-fluid mixutre will show little strength. The pore pressures dissipate rapidly. Deposition occurs in response to declining pore pressure. Deposition would take place rapidly from the base upward. Middleton and Hampton (1973, p. 14) refer to this mechanism as a gradual "freezing" from the base upward.

The sediment textures involved in such flows are clay, silt, and sand. Sediment concentrations are high, so only partial sorting and grading occurs (coarse-tail grading). Planar lamination and lensoid laminae may occur. Dish structures may form here due to loss of pore pressure and associated water escape, as suggested by both Middleton and Hampton (1973) and Lowe and LoPiccolo (1974).

The resulting sedimentary sequence is shown in Figure 88.

Turbidity Currents

A turbidity current is a turbulent mixture of sediment and water which is denser than the ambient fluid through which it moves, and is propelled by gravity. The support mechanism is fluid turbulence. In oceans and lakes, turbidity currents move as surges, being initiated by events like an earthquake, or slump failure, or gradation from fluidized sediment flow. The life span of the turbidity current is a function of the sediment volume that is entrained.

A turbidity current can be subdivided conveniently into a surging head, a neck and a body (Figure 89). Sediment is fed into the head region (Figure 89), although deposition takes place behind the head. When all the sediment is deposited, the current is dissipated. This process of deposition was observed experimentally by Middleton (1966 a, b, 1967) and confirmed by others.

In the marine environment, turbidity currents appear to occur and originate within submarine canyons. They also erode and form submarine canyons. The turbidity currents flow down canyon and then are channellized onto a submarine fan. Fan build-up occurs by channel extension in much the same way as a delta distributary extends and builds a delta. The turbidity currents become spread as thin sheets on the distal toe of submarine fans.

Komar (1969, 1972) has demonstrated that the flows are channellized and that the interchannel regions of a fan may receive sediment by overbank spill. In regions of higher slopes, flow is supercritical and overbank sedimentation occurs by rapid expansion of the head zone, and head-spill. Downslope, the flow becomes subcritical as slope angle declines, and overbank sedimentation occurs by body-spill.

In addition to being fed from the body and neck region, the head of a turbidity current may also act as a zone of erosion, with deposition immediately behind the head. Excess turbulence in the head may produce scour marks and sole marks which beomce filled rapidly.

The support mechanism for turbidity currents is fluid turbulence. The gravity driven motion of the fluid supplies excess turbulence which suspends the sediments. When these factors of gravity, suspension and turbulence are in equilibrium, the current system is considered to be in a stage of "autosuspension."

Deposition of sediment by turbidity currents is very rapid, particularly where there is a sudden reduction in slope, such as at the foot of a submarine canyon. Deposition may be rapid where there is a reduction in the degree of turbulence, or dissipation of energy by overbank, head or body spill.

The types of textures and structures occuring in turbidites (sediments deposited by turbidity currents) have been documented by many workers, and synthesized into a sequential model by Bouma (1962) who demonstrated that turbidity currents deposit sediments into a fining-upward sequence (Figures 88 and 90). A variety of tool marks and scour marks occur immediately at the base, including flute casts produced by turbulent scour, grooves produced by dragged objects and various prod, bounce and skip marks. These are overlain internally by a graded bed, overlain by parallel laminated sandstone, a micro-cross-laminated finer-grained sandstone and capped by an interval of interbedded siltstone and mudstone overlain by a pelagic clay. Load deformation structures including convolute laminae, load casts, pull aparts and slump folds may occur also.

HOLOCENE TURBIDITES

The best documentation of subaqueous gravity flows including turbidites, have come from studies of sediments known to have been deposited after an earthquake that triggered mass movements of sediment in the ocean floor. Many of these are associated with cable breaks for telecommunications. The best documented example is the 1929 Grand Banks Turbidity Current event (Figures 91, 92, 93) where velocities of 55 km per hour were determined from

time-distance curves.   Another example of a similar event,
with comparable data for velocities is the Orleansville,
Algeria, earthquake of 1954 (Heezen, 1963).

Turbidites tend to be commonly associated with
submarine   canyons,   submarine fans and abyssal plains
(Whitaker, 1974; Heezen, 1973).   Transport of sediment is
dispersed down canyon across submarine fans into abyssal
basins beyond the fan (Figure 94).   Within the canyon heads,
debris flow, grain flow and fluidized sediment flow tends to
be more common.   On the fans themselves, flow of turbidites
is channellized. The submarine fans are zoned (Figure 95)
according to slope, channel style and sediment distribution.
Normark (1969) showed that the apical portion of a fan is
cut by leveed channels, whereas the mid fan (or suprafan) is
traversed by distributary channel systems.   The distal toe
remains free of channels.   Fan build-up occurs by channel
extension and overbank spill, and by head spill or body
spill mechanisms (Griggs and Kulm, 1970; Nelson and Kulm,
1973; Komar, 1969, 1972).

A systematic change in texture and structures appears
to occur across a fan. The coarsest debris occurs in the
apical portion of the fan, and generally, grain size
decreases down fan.   However, no systematic change in
vertical sequences or style of Bouma sequences (Figure 99)
have   been   documented in submarine channels, despite
suggestions that such changes occur from analysis of ancient
sedimentary rocks.   Lateral changes in sequence appear
better to fit various overspill mechanisms (Figure 97).   The
geometry of fan channels is lenticular in section and linear
in plan with a distributary-type pattern (Figures 95, 96,
and 97 and 72).   The ocean basin floors are also sites of
turbidite sedimentation. The abyssal plains appear to be
basins, filled completely with turbidites, as indicated from
geophysical profiling. The marginal basins of the southwest
pacific are filled in part by turbidites, debris flow
conglomerates, and are arranged in coarsening-upward cycles
(Klein, 1975 a, b). Here the style of turbidite flows and
their stratigraphic position are interpreted to be in
response to sea floor spreading history of the basins.

ANCIENT TURBIDITES

Many ancinet turbidites have been documented in the
stratigraphic rock record, and only a partial listing will
be attempted here.   The Cenozoic and Cretaceous of Poland
(Carpathian Mountains), and the classic "Flysch" of the Alps
and the Appenines of Italy are few examples of ancient
turbidites. The Ordovician Martinsburg Formation (McBride,

1962) and the Ordovician Cloridorme Formation (Enos, 1969) of the Appalachians are well-documented examples. The California Coast Ranges are underlain by turbidites, especially the Pliocene of the Ventura Basin, and the Butano Sandstone (Eocene) of California (Nelson and Nilson, 1974; See also Figure 101). In the Gulf Coastal Plain, Whitaker (1974) refers to work by Bornhauser and Paine in the Oligocene and Miocene of Louisiana, in which submarine canyons are interpreted to be present. There, canyon fills acted as an unconformable seal on petroleum reservoirs. Walker (1975) has documented submarine channels in the Capistrano Formation (Miocene) of southern California (See also Moore and Fullam, 1975) (Figure 100).

In ancient turbidite basins, systematic changes in sediment properties have been recorded. Walker (1966, 1967) attempted to synthesize these changes in terms of lateral changes in the Bouma (1962) sequence (Figure 98). Along the proximal edge of a basin, the complete Bouma sequence should occur, and as one moves across the basin, the basal members progressively drop out as a turbidite loses its flow capacity. In the basin center (or distal zone) pelagic deposition should occur uninteruptedly. However, Griggs and Kulm (1970) demonstrated that no such systematic change occurs down slope in Cascadia Channel in the northeast Pacific (Figure 99), nor could it be demonstrated in an ancient example (Figure 101) by Nelson and Nilsen (1974). More recently, it has been recognized by Mutti and Ricci-Lucchi (1972) and Walker and Mutti (1973) that perhaps the best model for ancient turbidites is one of a progradation of a submarine fan (Figure 102). As the mid-fan overlaps the distal toe of a fan, and as the apical portion of a fan overlaps the mid fan, an overall coarsening-upward cycle should be generated. Several such coarsening-upward cycles have been documented in ancient flysch deposits (mutti and Ricci-Lucchi, 1972) and from deep-ocean marginal basins (Klein, 1975 a, b).

OIL FIELD EXAMPLES

The best oil field examples are in the Bakersfield area of California, the California continental shelf, and the Pliocene of California. Most of the hydrocarbon reservoir beds in the Sea of Japan, encountered during Leg 31 of the Deep Sea Drilling Project (Ingle, Karig et al, 1975) occur in turbidite beds. Future offshore drilling in deeper water is expected to exploit this environment further.

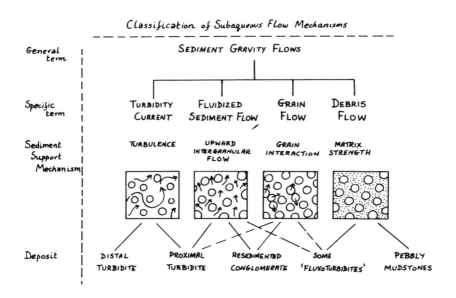

FIGURE 87. Classification of subaqueous flow mechanisms (From Middleton and Hampton, 1973; Reprinted by permission of the Pacific Section, Society of Economic Paleontologists and Mineralogists).

Sequence of Structures in hypothetical Single-mechanism Deposits.

Turbidity Current

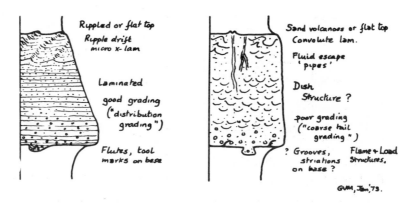

Rippled or flat top
Ripple drift micro x-lam

Laminated

good grading ("distribution grading")

Flutes, tool marks on base

Fluidized Flow

Sand volcanoes or flat top
Convolute lam.

Fluid escape 'pipes'

Dish Structure?

poor grading ("coarse tail grading")

? Grooves, striations on base?   Flame & Load Structures.

GVM, Jan '73.

Grain Flow.

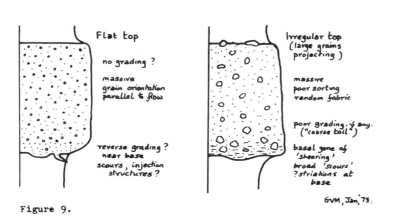

Flat top

no grading?

massive
grain orientation parallel to flow

reverse grading? near base
scours, injection structures?

Figure 9.

Debris Flow.

Irregular top (large grains projecting)

massive
poor sorting
random fabric

poor grading, if any. ("coarse tail")

basal zone of 'shearing'
broad 'scours'
?striations at base

GVM, Jan '73.

FIGURE 88. Vertical sequences of textures, sedimentary structures are surface contacts in hypothetical single-mechanism deposits produced by different type of subaqueous gravity flows (From Middleton and Hampton, 1973; Reprinted by permission of the Pacific Section, Society of Economic Paleontologists and Mineralogists).

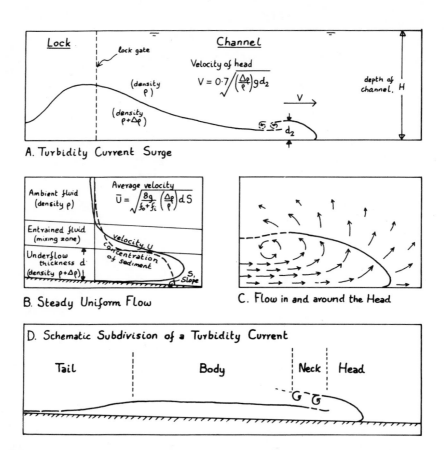

A. Turbidity Current Surge

B. Steady Uniform Flow

C. Flow in and around the Head

D. Schematic Subdivision of a Turbidity Current

FIGURE 89. Hydraulics of turbidity currents. A--turbidity current surge, as observed in a horizontal channel after releasing suspension from a lock at one end. The velocity of the head, v, is related to the thickness of the head, d_2, the density difference between the turbidity current and the water above, $\Delta\rho$, the density of the water, , and the acceleration due to gravity, g. B--steady, uniform flow of a turbidity current down a slope, s. The average velocity of flow, u, is related to the thickness of the flow, d, the density difference, and the frictional resistance at the bottom (f) and upper interface (f). C--flow pattern within and around the head of a turbidity current. D--Schematic division of a turbidity current into head, neck, body and tail. (From Middleton and Hampton, 1973; Reprinted by permission of the Pacific Section, Society of Economic Paleontologists and Mineralogists).

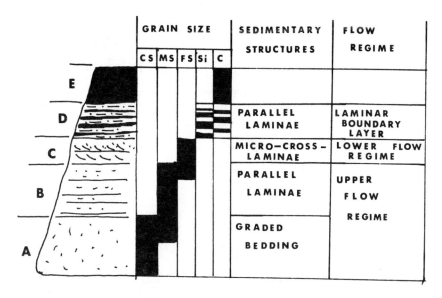

FIGURE 90. Bouma sequence of textures, lithologies and sedimentary structures in a typical turbidite. Letters refer to intervals proposed by Bouma (From Klein, 1972; after Bouma, 1962; Reprinted by permission from the Gological Society of America).

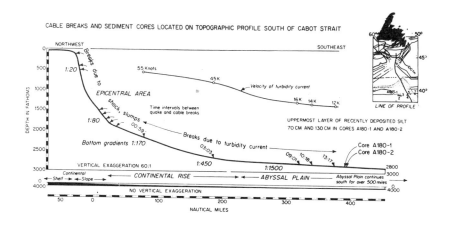

FIGURE 91. Profile over Grand Banks, Newfoundland, Turbidity Current showing position of cable breaks and velocity gradient of turbidity current (From Heezen, 1963; Reprinted by permission of John Wiley & Sons, Inc.)

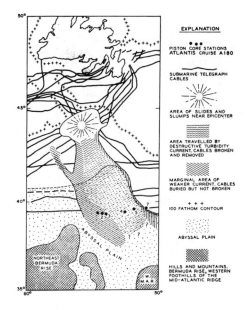

FIGURE 92. Map of 1929 Grand Banks Turbidity Current (From Heezen, 1963; Reprinted by permission of John Wiley & Sons, Inc.)

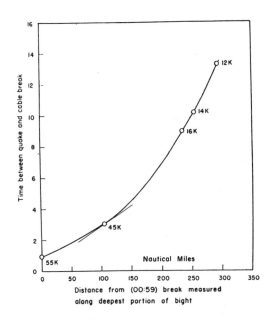

FIGURE 93. Time-distance plot of the 1929 Grand Banks turbidity current (From Heezen, 1963; Reprinted by permission of John Wiley and Sons, Inc.)

FIGURE 94. Routes of sediment dispersal from river mouth, through longshore currents into submarine canyon by gravity flows and turbidity currents to submarine fan on basin floor. Solid arrows show system of sand dispersal whereas dotted arrows show mud dispersal (From Moore, 1972; Reprinted by permission of the Geological Society of America.)

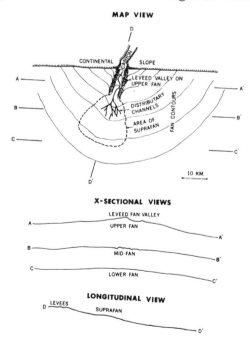

FIGURE 95. Model for growth of deep sea fan showing upper fan characterized by leveed fan valley, mid fan (or suprafan) characterized by distributaries, and absence of channels in distal portion of fan (From Normark, 1969; Reprinted by permission of the American Association of Petroleum Geologists.)

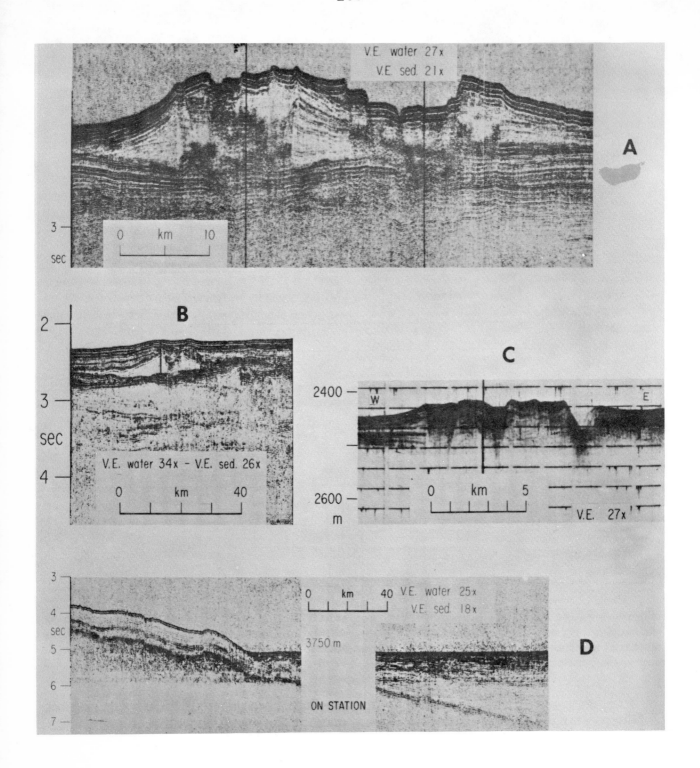

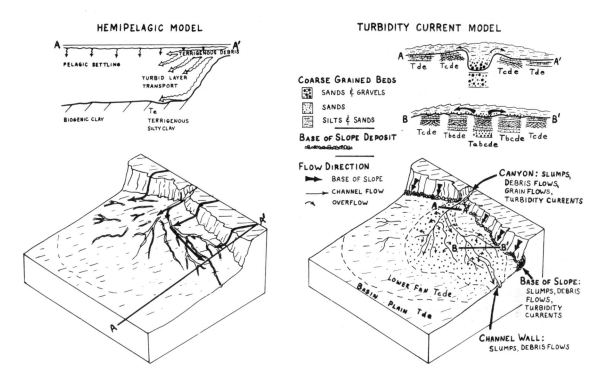

FIGURE 97. Models of hemipelagic and turbidity current processes on submarine fans. Cross-section AA' and BB' respectively show inferred sediment dispersal and lateral variation of Bouma (1962) sequence from channel floor to levee to inner fan regions (From Nelson and Kulm, 1973; Reprinted by permission of the Pacific Section, Society of Economic Paleontologists and Mineralogists).

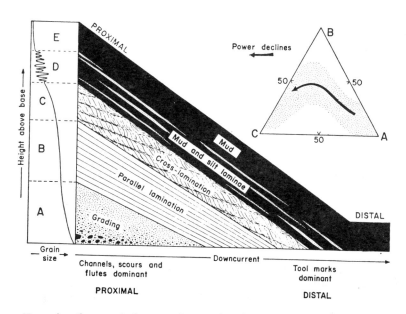

FIGURE 98. Vertical and lateral variation in downcurrent direction of an ideal turbidite bed (From Allen, 1970, after Walker, 1967).

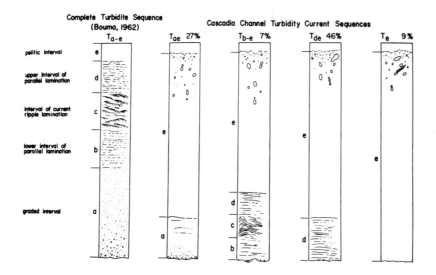

FIGURE 99. Sequences of sedimentary structures and textures from Cascadia Channel compared to ideal Bouma (1962) Sequence. Percentage of occurrence of various sequences in Cascadia Channel are indicated. Data base covers 90 percent of total sequences (From Griggs and Kulm, 1970; Reprinted by permission of the Geological Society of America).

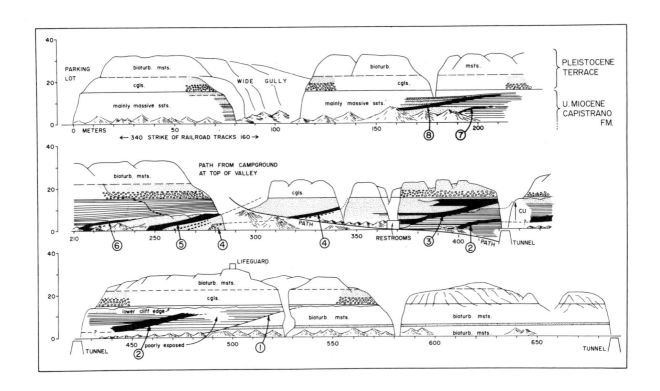

FIGURE 100. Cliff section at San Clemente, California, showing sketch of series of nested submarine channel fills, Capistrano Formation (Miocene). (From Walker, 1975; Reprinted by permission of the Geological Society of America.)

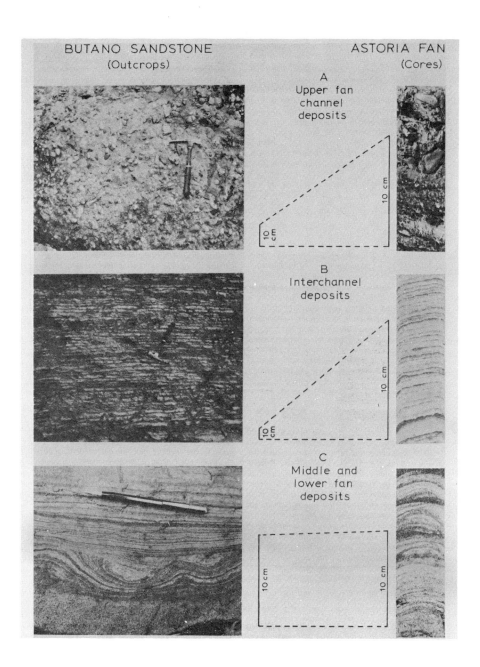

FIGURE 101. Comparison between sediment types and sedimentary structures of the Butano Sandstone (Eocene) on left and Astoria Fan (Right). (From Nelson and Nilsen, 1974; Reprinted by permission of the Society of Economic Paleontologists and Mineralogists.)

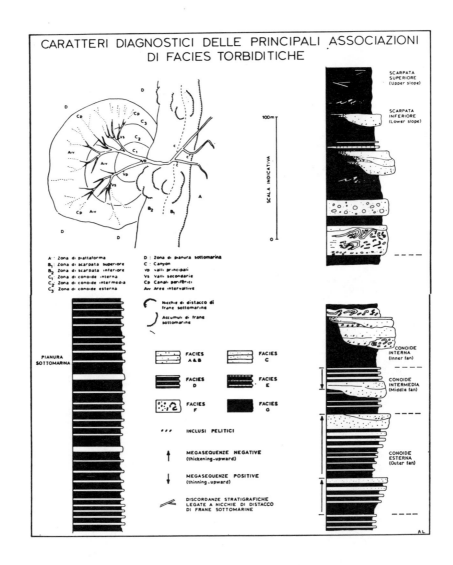

FIGURE 102. Normark (1969) model for submarine fan development (upper left) should be compared to Figure 71, and is used here as a predictive model to explain facies distributions in turbidite systems. Basinal facies shown in lower left, slope sequence in upper right, and series of coarsening-upward sequences produced by prograding submarine fan are shown in lower right (From Mutti and Ricci-Lucchi, 1972; Reprinted by permission of the Geological Society of Italy).

SELECTED BIBLIOGRAPHY

Bagnold, R.A., 1954, Experiments on a gravity-free dispersion of large solid spheres in a Newtonian fluid under shear: Roy. Soc. London Proc. Ser A., v. 225, p. 49-63.

Bouma, A.H., 1962, Sedimentology of some flysch deposits: Amsterdam, Elsevier, 169 p.

Curray, J.R. and Moore, D.G., 1971, Growth of the Bengal deep-sea fan and denudation of the Himalayas: Geol. Soc. America Bull., v. 82, p. 563-572.

Dill, R.F., 1964, Sedimentation and erosion in Scripps Submarine Canyon head, p. 23-41: in Miller, R.L. Editor, 1964, Papers in Marine Geology: New York, MacMillan Publishing Co.

Ewing, J.I., Ewing, M., Aitken, T., and Ludwig, W.J., 1968, North Pacific sediment layers measured by seismic profiling:, p. 147-173: in Knopoff, L., Drake, C.L., and Hart, P.J., editors, The Crust and upper mantle of the Pacific area: Am. Geophys. Union, Mon 12.

Griggs, B.G., and Kulm, L.V., 1970, Sedimentation in Cascadia deep-sea channel: Geol. Soc. America Bull., v. 81, p. 1361-1384.

Hampton, M.A., 1972, The role of subaqueous debris flow in generating turbidity currents: Jour. Sedimentary Petrology, v. 32, p. 775-793.

Heezen, B.C. and Ewing, M. 1952, Turbidity currents and submarine slumps, and the 1929 Grand Banks earthquake: Am. Jour. Sci., v. 250, p. 849-873.

Ingle, J.C. Jr., Karig, D.E., et al, 1973, Initial Report of the Deep Sea Drilling Project, v. 31: Washington, U.S. Government Printing Office.

Klein, G.deV, 1975a, Sedimentary tectonics in the southwest Pacific marginal basins based on Leg 30 deep sea Drilling Project cores from the South Fiji, Hebrides and Coral Sea Basin: Geol. Soc. America Bull., v. 86, p. 1012-1018.

_____, 1975b, Depositional facies of Leg 30 deep sea drilling project sediment cores: in Andrews, J.E., Packham, G, et al, In Press, Initial report of the Deep sea Drilling Project, v. 30: Washington, U.S. Government Printing Office.

Klein, G.deV, DeMelo, U., and Della Favera, J.C., 1972, Subaqueous
        gravity processes on the front of Cretaceous deltas, Roconcavo
        Basin, Brazil: Geol. Soc. America Bull., v. 83, p. 1469-1492.

Komar, P.D., 1969, The channellized flow of turbidity currents with
        application to Monterey deep-sea fan channel: Jour. Geophysical
        Research, v. 74, p. 4544-4558.

_____, 1972, Relative significance of head and body spill from
        a channelized turbidity current: Geol. Soc. American Bull.,
        v. 83, p. 1151-1156.

LaJoie, Jean, editor, 1970, Flysch sedimentology in North America:
        Geol. Assoc. Canada Spec. Paper No. 7.

Lowe, D.R., and LoPiccolo, R.D., 1974, The characteristics and
        origins of dish and pillar structures: Jour. Sedimentary
        Petrology, v. 44, p. 484-501.

McBride, E.F., 1962, Flysch and associated beds of the Martinsburg
        Formation (Ordovician), central Appalachians: Jour.
        Sedimentary Petrology, v. 32, p. 39-91.

Middleton, G.V., 1966a, Experiments on density and turbidity currents
        I. Motion of the head: Canadian Jour. Earth Sci., v. 3, p. 523-546.

_____, 1966b, Experiments on density and turbidity currents:
        II. Uniform flow of density currents: Canadian Jour. Earth
        Sci., v. 3, p. 627-637.

_____, 1967b, Experiments on density and turbidity currents:
        III. Deposition of sediment: Canadian Jour, of Earth Sc., v. 4,
        p. 475-506.

Middleton, G.V., and Hampton, M.A., 1973, Sediment gravity flows:
        mechanics of flow and deposition, p. 1-38: in Middleton, G.V.
        and Bouma, A.H., 1973, editors, Turbidites and deep-water
        sedimentation: Short course syllabus of Pacific Section, Soc.
        Econ. Paleontologists and Mineralogists, 157 p.

Moore, D.G., 1972, Reflection profiling studies of the California
        Borderland: structure and Quaternary turbidite basins: Geol.
        Soc. America Spec. Paper 107, 142 p.

Moore, G.T., and Fullam, T.J., 1975, Submarine channel systems and
        their potential for petroleum localization, p. 165-192: in Broussard,
        M.L., ediotr, 1975, Deltas 2nd Ed: Houston, Houston Geol. Soc.,
        555 p.

Mutti, E., and Ricci-Lucchi, F., 1972, Le torbiditi dell 'Appennino settentrionale: introduzione all 'analisi di facies: Mem. della Soc. Geologica Italiana, v. 11, p. 161-199.

Nelson, C.H., and Kulm, L.V., 1973, Submarine fans and channels, p. 39-78: in Middleton, G.V. and Bouma, A.H., 1973, editors, Turbidites and deep-water sedimentation: syllabus of Pacific Section, Soc. Econ. Paleontologists and Mineralogists, 157 p.

Nelson, C.H., and Nilsen, T.H., 1974, Depositional trends of modern and ancient deep sea fans, p. 69-91: in Dott, R.H., Jr., editor, 1974, Modern and ancient geosynclinal sedimentation: Soc. Econ. Paleontologists and Mineralogists Spec. Pub. 19, 380 p.

Normark, W.R., 1969, Growth patterns of deep-sea fans: Am. Assoc. Petroleum Geologists, v. 54, p. 2170-2195.

Stauffer, P.H., 1967, Grain-flow deposits and their implications, Santa Ynez Mountains, California: Jour. Sedimentary Petrology, v. 37, p. 487-508.

Walker, R.G., 1967, Turbidite sedimentary structures and their relationship to proximal and distal depositional environments: Jour. Sedimentary Petrology, v. 37, p. 25-43.

_____, 1973, Mopping up the turbidite mess. A history of the turbidity current concept., p. 1-37: in Ginsburg, R.N., 1973, Evolving concepts in sedimentology: Baltimore, John Hopkins Univ. Press., 191 p.

_____, 1975, Nested submarine-fan channels in the Capistrano Formation, San Clemente, Calfornia: Geol. Soc. America Bull., v. 86, p. 915-924.

Walker, R.G., and Mutti, E., 1973, Turbidite facies and facies associations, p. 119-158: in Middleton, G.V. and Bouma, A.H., editor, 1973, Turbidites and deep water sedimentation: Syllabus, Pacific Section, Soc. Econ. Paleontologists and Mineralogists, 157 p.

Whitaker, J.H., McD., 1974, Ancient submarine canyons and fan valleys, p. 106-125: in Dott, R.H., Jr., editor, 1974, Modern and ancient geosynclinal sedimentation: Soc. Econ. Paleontologists and Mineralogists Spec. Pub. no. 19, 380 p.